Bringing
the Story Home

Bringing
the Story Home

The Complete Guide

to Storytelling for Parents

by Lisa Lipkin

W · W · Norton & Company

New York   London

Portions of this work appeared in different form in *Family Circle* and *Parents*.

*Since this page cannot legibly accommodate all the copyright notices,
pages 220–21 constitute an extension of the copyright page.*

For information about permission to reproduce selections
from this book, write to Permissions,
W. W. Norton & Company, Inc., 500 Fifth Avenue, New York, NY 10110

The text of this book is composed in 11/14 Adobe Garamond
with the display set in ITC Kallos Book and Medium
Composition by Molly Heron
Manufacturing by The Courier Companies

Library of Congress Cataloging-in-Publication Data
Lipkin, Lisa.
Bringing the story home: the complete guide to storytelling for parents /
by Lisa Lipkin.
p.   cm.
Includes bibliographical references.
ISBN 0-393-04775-X
1. Storytelling. 2. Family recreation. I. Title.
LB1042.L515 2000

W. W. Norton & Company, Inc., 500 Fifth Avenue, New York, N.Y. 10110
www.wwnorton.com

W. W. Norton & Company Ltd., 10 Coptic Street, London WC1A 1PU

1   2   3   4   5   6   7   8   9   0

Contents

Preface

Most people search for a needle in a haystack. I'm just the opposite. I'm always looking for an entire haystack in the smallest of needles. I suppose you could say I like to find the story where none seems to exist. That's the main reason I decided to write this book—not to turn parents into fabulous storytellers (although if that happens as a result, I'll be delighted), but rather to help them elevate the mundane by finding the story that's lodged within it.

If you're open to them, stories exist everywhere. They're not limited to story hours at the library or at a storytelling festival. They don't live only in books, films, or television shows. They thrive in much subtler places, like in our eyes or our laugh lines, in the roughness of our hands or the lilt of our voices. They stow themselves in everyday places, like the walls of our homes or the streets where we live. They're perpetual children, playing hide-and-seek inside our family heirlooms and childhood toys. If we listened, really listened, to all the stories that surround us in our daily lives, the noise would be deafening.

This book is about using stories to transform the ordinary in your lives into the extraordinary. Hopefully, by providing a more "storied" home, you'll become a more creative, communicative family. At the very least, you'll have a lot of fun trying. To a culture that increasingly relies on external devices to entertain, storytelling is the perfect rebuttal.

When I look back over the stories in my life that had a profound effect on me, I realize there are far too many to enumerate. A few that are constant companions are worth sharing with you. The first is a story told to me by my mother, when I was a senior in high school and under a lot of self-imposed pressure to get into college. "You know," she said to me in her thick Hungarian accent, "I heard about a boy who applied to several average colleges and got rejected from all of them." "And this is supposed to make me feel better?" I asked her. "Wait, there's more," she said. "After the boy received all of his rejection letters, his father said to him, 'Now, aim higher.' So the boy applied to Harvard and he got in." Shortly thereafter, I stuck an application in the mail to a top women's college and was accepted, even though the lesser schools had rejected me. In retrospect, I realize her story wasn't about colleges at all, but about human nature. Sometimes it takes a top-notch thinker to recognize in us what more mediocre minds can't.

Her story stayed with me and on more than one occasion helped steer the course of my life. Years after college, I decided to try my hand at journalism. I submitted a story proposal to a small, regional newspaper in New Jersey, where I was living at the time. Needless to say, it was rejected. For a moment, I lost heart and considered sending my story idea to an even smaller publication in the area, thinking it would have a greater chance of being published. But then I recalled my mother's story and decided to send my proposal to the *New York Times* instead. They bought it immediately, and I was on my way to becoming a published writer.

Like most teenagers, my adolescent years were filled with self-doubt and anxiety, masked by noisy self-assurance. I talked incessantly at the dinner table, mugged for family photos, and acted in every school play in which I was cast. But underneath that veneer of confidence loomed a fragile sixteen-year-old who felt misunderstood by her parents and overlooked by boys her own age.

One summer, I got a job selling T-shirts on Cape Cod. For the most part, the customers consisted of blue-haired, tour bus ladies and families whose restless children inevitably deposited a portion of their ice cream cones on the merchandise. One afternoon, after an exhausting day in the sweltering heat (the owner hadn't heard of air-conditioning), a man in his forties walked into the store. For the life of me, I can't remember his face, only what he said. The two of us began a conversation and within a matter of minutes, it veered off in many delicious directions. We spoke of art and artists we both admired; of Vladimir Nabokov and Dorothy Parker, my two favorite writers of that time; of his travels to Alaska and beyond. Then, out of nowhere, the man said, "You're very special. I'd like to share a story with you before I leave . . .

Michelangelo was walking down the street with his friend one day. As they passed a rock on the side of the road, the friend playfully kicked it. "Why did you kick that?!!" Michelangelo inquired, quite incensed. "What's the big deal?" his friend replied. "It's just a rock." "No, " Michelangelo said. "it's an angel." Several months later, Michelangelo invited his friend to his studio where he unveiled his newest sculpture. It was a beautifully carved angel. When his friend marveled at it, Michelangelo said, "You see, I told you it wasn't a rock."

Suddenly, the man turned to me and said, "So what I'm trying to tell you is that you're an angel, and most people will just see the rock." And he turned around and left the store. A virtual stranger handed me a gift that I've carried with me ever since.

In many ways, the two stories I've mentioned are variations on the same theme. Reach higher. Have faith in your gifts. Be strong. It's no coincidence that the stories I most need to hear are the ones that I remember the most vividly.

Important stories stick. They can't be contrived but they can be conjured. It all begins with you, the master magician. The stories you elicit might not be lengthy, they might not even be more than a sentence, but some of those images will make important etchings on your children's imaginations. They'll remember them long after you put away your wizard's wand.

Nowhere in this book will you find instructions on how to "perform" stories. I won't suggest that you turn out the lights, don fancy costumes, or reach for your bag of props, because I truly believe that the way stories can have a lasting impact on you and your children is through their daily application, not as a "special performance hour." Ironic, coming from a professional storyteller. But even those of us who do this for a living know that the source of our inspiration comes not from our big moments on stage, but from our day-to-day observations and musings.

Several months ago my dear friend Steve Zeitlin, a folklorist who knows how to find every interesting subculture in New York, introduced me to a smoky table-tennis club on the West Side of Manhattan. The club, filled with closet Ping-Pong fanatics, also attracts the Who's Who of the sport. There's Marty Reisman, who won the British Open in 1949; Dick Miles, a ten-time United States champion; and George Braithwaite, one of the fellows sent by our government to play Ping-Pong with the Chinese, just before Nixon opened up relations with that country. All of these guys had only one thing to say about my backhand: "Change your grip!!"

But how could I? I had a wicked forehand, honed during my childhood years playing "basement Ping-Pong" in our home in New Jersey. However, I realized that my forehand grip made it impossible to switch effectively to my backhand, so I worked on developing a new grip for months, to no avail. "Give it time," they all said, adamant in their advice.

Then, something interesting happened. Monica Golusevic, a former Romanian national champion, wandered into the club one day. "Why don't you show me the grip that you're most comfortable with?" she said. So I did. "You know," she said, "there's a British champion who uses your grip." "Really?" I said. She reassured me and said, "Why don't you and I work on developing your backhand using the grip you're used to and comfortable with?" I felt as if a ton of bricks had just been lifted from my head. But I knew the relief I felt went beyond Ping-Pong. It suddenly occurred to me that the best teachers aren't the ones who try to turn people into something they aren't, but instead they are the ones who try to make the most out of the gifts people already have. It's an important lesson, and one that hopefully translates onto the following pages.

Trust in your natural storytelling gifts. Trust in your children's unyielding capacity to create, enjoy, and listen to the stories you tell them. Use this book like you would a Stairmaster. It's not going to turn you into a six-foot model with impeccable abs, but it will strengthen your imaginative muscle. You don't need to jump around like a professional storyteller in order to be effective. Simply be yourself, and your stories, and those of your family, will emerge gracefully, naturally, and with joyous abundance.

Acknowledgments

The writing of a book is a huge story in and of itself. Some of the more important characters in this behind-the-scenes tale include Lisa and Andrew Meade, who generously donated their extra bedroom in the countryside for me to write in, thereby liberating me from the noisy garbage trucks of 10th Avenue. Steve Zeitlin, a wonderful folklorist and founder of City Lore in Manhattan, entered the story at around Chapter 6, when I started calling him every five minutes with questions about permissions and rights to material. My father, George Lipkin, helped drive the plot by answering countless questions on grammar, and my mother, Sari Lipkin, created the story structure years ago through her animated musings about everyday life. My agent, Naomi Wittes Reichstein, patiently helped me start this story, and my delightful editor, Amy Cherry, helped me end it. To all of you, I offer sincerest thanks.

Introduction

A man is always a teller of tales, his lives surrounded by his stories and the stories of others, he sees everything that happens to him through them; and he tries to live his life as if he were telling a story.
JEAN-PAUL SARTRE

It's not easy being a frog, particularly when you have to entertain three hundred irrepressible children. But years of performance experience have taught me how to control my audience, and things seemed to be going my way last spring at a public school in Brooklyn when, dressed as giant green frog, I spun an original story, while dancing and rapping my way toward environmental awareness. "*Ribbut-Ribbut-Ribbut-Ugh. Ribbut-Ribbut-Ribbut-Ugh. Oh Yeah, Ugh Ugh,*" I called out, as the giggling children clapped and sang along with me. Suddenly, out of the corner of my Styrofoam eyehole, I spotted the principal marching down the aisle and heading to the front of the auditorium. She was screaming something at me and breaking the concentration of the kids.

"Miss!" she shouted. I stopped singing. The rap beat continued to play on without me. I stood in silence as all my childhood fears came tumbling back. I was in trouble with the principal.

"Yes?" I said meekly.

"You forgot to leave your parking pass with the front office. Could you get it for me please?" she said casually.

What could I do? I danced over to my bag, hidden behind the giant cardboard tree, and plunged my webbed fingers into it. Three hundred pairs of eyes were fixed upon me as I fished around to the rhythms of the beat, continuing to bump and grind my gills as I excavated the parking permit from my bag and handed it to her. Once satisfied, she marched away, leaving an audience of perplexed children, mouths hanging open in confusion, for me to appease.

An unlikely scenario? Unfortunately, it's not. I can barely remember the last time a school performance of mine wasn't interrupted. Sometimes it's an oblivious school janitor, marching a ladder across the stage. Other times it's a blaring announcement, coming through a classroom's intercom. Often enough, it's the teachers, issuing directives to students while they are creating a story. And yet we complain about the ailing attention spans of our children. We bemoan their decreasing imaginations. We mourn their lack of respect for others. And yet we continue to interrupt our children's stories.

As a professional storyteller, I've traveled across America, running workshops and performances for audiences of every age and socioeconomic background. If there's one universal thread that binds all people together, it's their need for stories. Not in broken increments, and not only as entertainment or as a diversion from the world, but as an essential life force.

Since the time we enter this world, we live in stories, inhaling and exhaling them. They are inherent in everything we do. They're implicit in our casual greetings, like "Hey, what's happening?," "Wait until I tell you what I saw at school!, " or "What did you hear about her?" They're in the anecdotes spun at a family picnic, a dinner table, or a car trip, or in the symbols we surround ourselves with: a diamond ring, a patchwork quilt, a Bar Mitzvah gift. They're even in television. Indeed, exchanging stories is our most basic and primitive instinct.

Stories are how we learn, a fact our ancestors understood. When prehistoric man gathered in tribal groups, around a roaring fire, it was their shared stories that reunited them each night and strengthened their communal bond. In retelling the events of the day, or recalling an ancient epic, passed down over centuries, they taught young men how to hunt and women how to care for their young. They comforted the sick, by reminding them of those who were healed before or of those who had conquered pain. In lieu of modern medicine they administered the spoken word, applying humorous anecdotes to the wound, bandaging it with metaphors. They understood that in stories lay wisdom. Without them, they would be lost as individuals and as a tribe.

But one hardly needs to look to the Stone Age to find remnants of an oral culture. Even to our parents and grandparents, storytelling was part of an everyday routine. It happened when they went around the corner to buy a fresh loaf of bread, and the baker, covered in flour, asked, "How are things?" Or on sweltering nights, when everyone in the neighborhood sat outside on their porches, in the park, or on their stoops and simply gossiped. They would exchange stories with the family physician, who knew their medical histories and family secrets, or heed the warning of the pharmacist, who recalled for them an incident in which a drug wasn't used properly. They would stay glued to the radio on Saturday mornings for "Let's Pretend," a bacchanalia of fairy tales and adventure stories, or follow the midday tribulations of "Our Gal Friday," whose narrator dramatically asked listeners each week, "Can a girl from a small mining town find happiness as the wife of a wealthy English nobleman?" Storytelling was woven into the mundane aspects of their lives, and to them it was as natural as breathing.

Yet in the short span of a generation, the oral tradition has virtually evaporated from our workaday world. Instead, we've replaced our stories with sound bites and fragmented behavior that manifests itself every day in small and subtle ways: the cashiers who haven't finished serving one customer before they're on to the next; conversationalists who prefer looking everywhere but at the person who is speaking to them; television shows that cut to a new angle every tenth of a second; and school assemblies interrupted by those who should know better.

Now, more than ever, parents need to reintroduce stories into their children's lives. In an age without extended families and tight community bonds, when the arts are being cut systematically from school budgets, and computers and televisions are usurping the majority of our days, stories are our antidote.

The stories we tell our children will define who they are and where they are heading. More important, they will teach our kids to dream. I've seen the imaginations of children soar when I've asked them to create a story. I've observed learning disabled children transcend their school-appointed labels and painfully shy kids transform into confident yarn spinners. I've witnessed the pure joy that clings to their faces when I tell children a story.

The chapters in this book are designed to bring stories back into your lives and the lives of your children. Hopefully, they will remind you of your own boundless imagination in the process. Whether you want to read aloud or simply tell a story from your past, there will be something in the following pages for you.

PHILOSOPHY AND APPROACH

One of my first professional jobs as a storyteller was with the New York City Board of Education. Each week I was expected to travel to a different classroom throughout the city, where I would run interactive storytelling workshops for grammar school students. Naturally, I planned my programs weeks ahead of time and created the perfect scenario in my mind: My sessions would take place in a special story corner in the back of each classroom. Certain students would act out stories through movement. Others would don masks and costumes. If time permitted, we would accompany the story with musical instruments. It seemed like the perfect program. Then I entered reality.

Story corner?! I was lucky if I got a square foot at the front of the room. Schools were hopelessly overcrowded. Classrooms were minute, and class sizes were overwhelming. Often there would be close to forty kids in a room built for half as many. All my plans went down the drain. And it was the best thing that could have happened to me.

Since there were no extra supplies, the students and I had no costumes, props, or any other accoutrements to use. Because there wasn't one drop of extra space, the children were forced to sit at their desks. But to my surprise, the children compensated for their lack of square footage by creating acres of land in their heads. What we couldn't manufacture literally, we did through our imaginations. If I needed a twelve-foot bird, the students would automatically stretch out their arms and become one. If my story called for a basket full of apples, they simply reached under their desks and grabbed it. If a character in my story needed to run around the room, they would move their heads and their hands in a circle, while still sitting in their seats! The less they had physically, the more they reached for mentally.

There was another added bonus to our lack of mobility: By keeping the children at their desks, I was inadvertently sending them an important message: *Creative time is not separate from work time. It is an integrated part of your studies. Imagination and creativity should not be relegated to an arts and crafts hour or a story corner. It should live among your books, within your math equations, alongside your everyday routines.* That is this book's prevailing philosophy, and one that I hope will enter into your homes in the same way it entered into the New York City school system.

We've been conditioned to believe that storytelling has to be an event, complete with drums and sparkling shoes. But by treating it as "entertainment" we trivialize it. I'd rather see you and your children view stories as a natural process. That's why I don't put much emphasis in this book on the peripherals, like choosing the correct space, the perfect setting, or the ideal atmosphere.

Naturally a quiet room with soft lighting can make a wonderful environment for storytelling, and if you can take the time to make an event out of storytelling once in a while, your kids will undoubtedly love it. But I'm less interested in storytelling as performance and more interested in it as life. Would you make a special ritual out of brushing your teeth? Would you gather round in a circle when serving a meat loaf? I doubt it. So why treat storytelling any differently? I believe that only when storytelling becomes mundane can it really penetrate family life.

When my father told me his most affecting stories, they weren't during "story hour." They were while he was opening a can of peas or changing a lightbulb. His stories tumbled out naturally, and I absorbed them naturally too. They entered my soul like a cool drink of lemonade on a summer's day, smoothly, without being contrived, cajoled, or manufactured.

This book isn't about making you a great storyteller, although that would be nice. It's about getting you to start the storytelling process at home and about integrating imagination and stories into all aspects of your family life. Maybe that will mean one five-minute activity once a year. Or maybe it will enter your home on a regular basis. Don't feel you have to be a theater major or an English literature buff to be successful at these exercises. Whatever your temperament, even if you're a bookish science type or a retiring wallflower, you still have the ability to make storytelling come alive at home.

Stories can and should be part of your routine. That's why virtually all of the activities in this book can be done while attending to your normal schedule. They can be used while eating dinner, while driving your kids to school, while cooking a meal. They can happen over the course of an hour or during a thirty-second commercial break. They can enhance your kids' academic studies or help you read aloud more effectively. They can provide your children with an alternative to television and a remedy for boredom. Best of all, they will help you see that you can cull a story from just about anywhere, at any time.

The activities in this book were developed over the last twelve years through trial and error, in classrooms, at festivals, during workshops, in community centers, and in private homes. As silly as some of the exercises may seem on first reading, they work for almost all families. Push yourselves to try them. You will be amazed by how easily you master them and how eager your kids are to participate. You'll also find story boxes throughout the book in which parents share their favorite storytelling ideas and activities.

This book is as much about helping you to reclaim your own imaginations as it is about stimulating your children's. In trusting your own capacity to cull stories from the simplest places, in believing in your ability to find an entire haystack in the smallest of needles, you will have made lifelong changes in the way your family communicates together.

Bringing
the Story Home

1

Making a Mountain out of a Molehill

Integrating Storytelling into Everyday Activities

*A skilled storyteller not only maneuvers imaginations around
interruptions and over inconsistencies, transforming breakfast nooks
into banquet halls, pots of geraniums into rain forests; he convinces a
group of people to travel to those secret, fabulous places without the
use of slides, or maps, or souvenirs.*
EDITH HAZARD, *Singing for Your Supper*

I grew up in northern New Jersey, in a sleepy, suburban community. Outside our home, the manicured lawns and neatly groomed
sidewalks painted a portrait of pristine serenity. Inside, however,
things weren't nearly as contained.

The impending storm usually arrived at dinnertime. Everyone
talked at once. No one listened. We gabbed, laughed, gesticulated,
and ate simultaneously. Food, chaos, and endless stories swirled
around us, enveloping us in a kind of sweet madness. Friends who
occasionally came for supper were stunned, their mouths hanging
open in confusion. They'd never seen anything like it: the never-

ending stream of aromas and tastes, the endless supply of stories, each family member competing for attention. Funny thing is, they usually left smiling.

Meals rarely ended without a story, a juicy anecdote, or a word game. Our folly wasn't contrived. My parents never said to us, "Now, we'll have a story hour or joke time before you kids go up to bed." They simply couldn't help themselves. They had stories to tell, gossip to share, things to talk about. They grew up in storied homes, where singing and game playing were part of a dinner hour. They were simply sharing with my brother and me what came naturally. And it was the best gift they could have given us. Our dinner soirees bonded us as a family and excited us about the dazzling world of language and ideas. Best of all, they taught us how to entertain ourselves.

Of course, times have changed. These days, you're more likely to find a television set than a *raconteur* sitting in your kitchen. Even if an eccentric uncle, bursting with stories, were waiting at home for you, who would have the time to listen to him? *Free time* has almost become an oxymoron. Between car pools and children's ballet lessons, soccer practice, and homework, there simply isn't any more time in a day. That's why the activities in this chapter are designed to fit in with your normal daily routine. You don't have to take one extra minute out of your day to use them. Simply integrate the activities in this chapter into whatever you've already planned for your family. Use them at meals. Try them while you're tidying up, or even when you're chauffeuring your kids to a friend's house.

Remember, the goal of this book is to encourage you to see storytelling not as performance art, but as life. Don't save the activities in this chapter for a rainy day. Use them all the time like condiments, to spice up your child's existing hobbies and habits. If you treat storytelling as if it were the most natural thing in the world, eventually it will be.

MEALTIME

The dining table is the first place to start, since it's the place the family naturally gathers each day and where a routine is already established. Where do you begin? Do you announce to your kids your intentions to do storytelling? Do you gather them in a special room? On the contrary, you do nothing out of the ordinary. Simply sit down at the dinner table as you normally would. Talk and eat as you always do. The storytelling should embellish, not replace, your existing conversation.

> My son was a lousy eater. The only way I could get him to have dinner was by telling him a story. I'd say, "Come on, I want to tell you a story!" He would be so mesmerized by my tale, his mouth would hang open and I would push food into it. He didn't even know he was eating.
>
> ROSLYN BRESNICK PERRY, STORYTELLER

At a point when there's a lull in the conversation, simply ask your kids (and spouse) to become an object on the dinner table. You might say to them, "If you could become any object on this table, what would you be?" Go around the table and have everybody introduce themselves, announcing which object they are. "I'm a carrot stick." "I'm the salt shaker." "I'm the orange juice that spilled on the table." Then start the ball rolling by asking each child to describe what his or her life is like as that object. Once things get moving, have your children take turns asking each other questions.

Initially your kids may have some trouble coming up with ideas, particularly if they're not used to this kind of play at home. Help them along by asking them probing questions. You might say, "As the tablecloth, how does it feel to have juice spilled right on top of you?" "If you're a cup, do you get along with your saucer?" "Have you heard any gossip while in the dishwasher?" "What's it like being swished around in there?"

Don't ask only visual questions. Focus on scents, tastes, and textures too. For example, you may want to ask your son, the pepper grinder, "What do mashed potatoes feel like when you're sprinkled on them?" Or you might ask your daughter, the drinking glass, "What taste gives you the most joy when it's in you?" The more inventive and probing your questions are, the more creative their answers will be.

Don't be discouraged if your children greet this activity with cynicism. They may have their defenses up, particularly if they aren't used to this kind of storytelling. Persevere! With a little encouragement, it won't take long for them to come around and fully participate.

What Do I Do If One of My Kids Acts Up?

Try making him or her the star character. Reticence is more a cry for attention than a sign of disapproval. Once your child is center stage, he or she will revel in the new-found character.

The important thing to remember is to not make a big deal out of the activity. Serve it to your kids like you would a new yummy dessert. At first, they may cringe, but once they taste it, they'll ask for it all the time.

Can I Use This Activity in Other Contexts?

Absolutely. In fact, this activity can be a wonderful teaching tool. The next time you're out for a walk with your kids, point to a tree and have them become objects on it. Depending on the time of year, they might choose to be a branch, a leaf, or even a squirrel. Ask them to share their stories with you. Not only will the activity be fun, but also they'll be studying nature in the process.

Or use it to learn about history. Instead of becoming an object on your dinner table, ask your children to become objects on George Washington's dinner table. Even if your kids don't know much about Colonial dining habits, they'll certainly learn about them from this game. And you can guide them by asking historical questions that help them understand the time period. For example, you might say to one of your children, "Tell me, as a dinner plate, were you hand painted?" Or, "I see you've chosen to become a silver candle stick. Were you made by a local silversmith?" "As the homemade bread, tell us your personal story—how did you get made? Was it difficult? Or was it a pleasant adventure?"

Approach mealtime with a sense of fun.

Wear a Magical Necktie to Lunch. It may not be the dress code in the middle of the day but it certainly helps kids sit through a meal. Start by grabbing an imaginary tie out of the air and fastening it around your neck. Describe it to your kids. Perhaps it's decorated with food, so if you spill something, no one can tell. Perhaps it belongs to a prince from a faraway kingdom. If so, tell everyone about the tie's journey—how it got there, why it decided to run away from the palace, and how you plan to help the tie return home. Then have your kids do the same.

Make Dinner a Feast of Fun and Games. Have your children invite a mystery guest from a familiar storybook to dinner. Everyone at the table takes turns asking questions about the guest (Is it a girl with red hair? Is she from a fairy tale?) until the character is identified. Then let your children set a place for the guest and serve her all her favorite foods.

Make a Gigantic, Invisible Cake for Dessert One Night. While "baking" it, have your children fish through a make–believe mixing bowl and encourage them to feel the ingredients. Is it filled with bowling ball–sized cherries? Walnuts as big as houses? Look!

There's someone inside! Ask him what he wants, and share his unusual story with everyone at the table.

What Happens If My Kids Can't Visualize It?

Chances are, if your children can't see the imaginary object, it is because you can't. Children will follow your lead but they know when their parents are faking it, so take the exercise seriously! If I refer to an imaginary object during my performance, you better believe that forty-five minutes later, when the show is over, the kids in the audience will ask me what happened to that object. They can still see it and they believe in its presence. So before you reach for an imaginary object, you must make a commitment to yourself that you will see the entire episode through from beginning to end. Thus, if you lift an imaginary pink elephant out of the cake, you can't just let your hands drop five minutes later when the phone rings. Or if you do, make sure you tell the kids to grab the tusks, before the two-ton beast runs amok in the kitchen. In other words, see it and believe it!

HOUSEHOLD CHORES

Turn Vacuuming into an Adventure. Tell your children to pretend they're a giant king from the land of Dustabaloo who loves to eat dust! Each time they vacuum they are, in actuality, feeding his enormous appetite for dirt and dust. Tell them to move with the vacuum as a hungry king would and to narrate his story while they clean.

While Your Children Are Loading the Dishwasher, Suggest That They Become One of the Objects in It! Have them tell their story of being swished around or of going through the rinse and dry cycles and of being squeaky clean. Once they're done with their task, they can act out the whole wash cycle for one another, by playing different objects as they go through their very wet adventure.

Make Cleanup Fun. Ask your kids to imagine how the objects in their room must feel now that they are getting put back where they belong. Are they relieved to be back on the shelf with their old familiar friends? Have your children describe the thoughts and personal stories of those objects.

Dress for the Mess. Cleaning one's room is much more fun when you can wear a silly object atop your head. Why not have your children reach into their ears and pull a Messy Mop Hat out and wear it? Perhaps they'll put on a magic Speed Visor, which will help them work faster to get the job done. Maybe they'll even put a song hat on your head, which can sing along with them while they tidy your room.

Storytelling helps me not get reactive with my son when he does something that really annoys me. For example, when I'm trying to get him to take a bath and he's resistant, I'll use a story trick. I'll say, "You don't have to take a bath with me. I'll just take a bath with this toy duck—it told me that it has a funny story to tell." As soon as I start turning the conflict into a storytelling adventure, I forget that I'm angry. You can't be creative and mad at the same time.

BERTA FRANK, mother of Zev, 3, and Elizabeth, 1

Keep Your Child Occupied While You Are Cooking. Tell your children to take out the enormous invisible storybook that's in the refrigerator. Clear away a space for it on the counter and make sure you point out its large size and heavy weight. Then ask your children to read you the story, page by page.

What Happens If My Child Can't See Any Text?

Assume that your child can't see anything because that particular page is blank. Have your child describe the illustration on the following page instead. Or, ask why the book is blank. Is it a mystery book that needs to be decoded? Maybe the two of you should sprinkle some magic (invisible) paprika on it, so that the words will appear. Always accept your child's answers and build on them.

INSTEAD OF TV

> My sister and I used to play in the house on Saturday morning because girls weren't allowed to go out as much. And she's the one who said, "You know, there's a city behind the television." See, these old televisions used to have the cardboard (backs) with holes in them. The television was on and we could see all of the lights on in the back. I remember the structure: there were big tubes on the left and big tubes on the right and these tiny tubes in the middle. So we took the cardboard off and put our dolls in there and played that it was the city of Manhattan. It was our own doll's house.
>
> ISABEL ALVAREZ,
> from *City Play* by Steve Zeitlin and Amanda Dargan

Instead of Using Your Remote Control to Turn on the Television, Use It to Turn on Your Children's Imagination. Have your kids become a button on the television remote control pad—maybe they're a VIDEO/VCR button, maybe they're the VOLUME CONTROL. Ask them to describe their story and why they do or don't like their job.

Create Your Own Talk Show. Have your child become the host of a talk show, where the guests are objects in nature instead of people. Ask him to play the host and interview a tree, a flower, or even poison ivy! Just like on television, have him go into the audience and ask if anyone has any questions they'd like to ask the guest. If someone chooses to be a weed, have the weed tell its story. Look who the mystery guest is! It's a giant fern! Make sure the audience hears his amazing story!

Pretend You're a Television Actor Looking Out from Your Television Set at the Audience. Have the children talk to the viewers and tell them what they are thinking and seeing from inside the tube. If your son becomes Bart Simpson, have him describe the most memorable story that happened on the set. If your daughter is Barney, have her tell what's it like working with all those kids!

BEDTIME

Make the Blanket a Magic Carpet. Once the children are tucked in and ready for bed, have them pull up their enchanted covers. Everyone knows that magic covers like to travel once the lights are out. Where will your children's blankets be going tonight? Will they go along for the ride? If so, have them tell you about their intended journey.

Stop by the Wallpaper Cafe. Everyone knows that the patterns in wallpaper have a lively social hour when humans leave the room. Have your kids eavesdrop on their conversations. If your wallpaper has flowers in it, describe what two buds are talking about. Maybe there's a stripe and a check engaged in an intense discussion at a coffee bar. Have fun and your kids will be sure to follow.

Become Your Favorite Sleepy Character. How does Sleeping Beauty look when she sleeps? What about the three little pigs? Ask your child to imitate the way his favorite storybook characters would sleep. Have him also demonstrate the way his favorite characters would talk in their sleep, snore, or wake up.

Make Sleepy Time Magic Time. Bedtime can be a whole lot better once you ask your child to reach into her magic pillow case and pull out something ridiculous. Maybe it's a pepperoni pizza with peppers and purple porpoises. Maybe it's a three-thousand-foot skyscraper. Be careful though. It's so tall it's poking a hole in the ceiling! Have your child make up a story about the objects she pulls out of the magic pillow case.

TRAVEL

Long trips by car or air can be difficult for younger children, since they don't have the freedom to run around. Storytelling and make-believe games can be a wonderful alternative to board games or an in-flight movie. Children can do the following activities right in their seats.

Pretend the Inside of the Car Is a Movie Studio. Now have the kids create their own feature film. Instead of people, however, have the stars be the objects in the car. Ask one child to play the snobby steering wheel, and another play the dainty windshield wiper, or even the tuna sandwich on the front seat. Become the director and yell "Action!" as each character individually performs a monologue about its life.

Have Your Kids Become Famous Detectives. Ask them to decipher the code being sent to them by the plane's wing. What adventure story is the wing trying to share with the passengers? Is it complaining about being tickled by the clouds? Is a bird annoying it? Have them find out the wing's secret story and share it.

Make the Most out of a Seat Pocket. It may hold magazines and safety instructions, but there's magic in there too! Have your child reach deep inside it and pull out something imaginary! Maybe it's a talking horse or a dancing dinosaur. Maybe there's an imaginary storybook in there. Take it out and read it aloud!

Stay in Style While Traveling. It may not be proper to wear your hat inside a restaurant, but everyone needs a good motoring cap. Have your kids put on their "car hats," then describe them to you. Perhaps your son has a "shiny steering wheel hat," or your daughter is wearing a "road map hat." If that's the case, perhaps she can help you navigate. You can combine these games with practical safety considerations too. For example, you can tell your children that driving hats only appear after seat belts are fastened, since all magic driving caps are safety conscious. Or they appear only when the kids are speaking quietly, since soft-spoken driving hats don't have the courage to emerge when there is shouting in the car. Do the same for plane travel, using commonly found objects on a plane as your guide. Perhaps your daughter is wearing a dinner tray hat. Watch out! The melting cheese is dripping down her nose! Or maybe your son is wearing a crown. Quick, everyone bow to the king of American Airlines!

MORE FUN MAGIC CAPS

On Holidays. Why not add excitement to festival days by wearing a special holiday hat? Perhaps you're wearing a Christmas wreath on your head. Be careful! A piece of evergreen is tickling your nose! Maybe you're wearing a Chanukah menorah on your head. Oh no.

One of the candles just melted on your ear! And as for Thanksgiving, Dad sure looks funny with a giant turkey leg hanging off his head.

On Rainy Days. Rainy day hats are always fun, since they sing and dance and keep you entertained when the weather makes going outside impossible. Put on your rainy day caps and watch the magic happen. Show each other what your rainy day cap has given you the power to do. I bet you didn't know that various members of your family could tap-dance, sing out of tune while bicycling with their feet up in the air, or speak ancient Chinese and contemporary Pig Latin! It's amazing what a rainy day hat will do for your day.

On Sick Days. Sick days are no fun, but hats make them a little bit better. Why not have your child wear a massage hat, and have her close her eyes and feel it massaging her shoulders and aching tummy?

HOMEWORK

Storytelling can enhance your child's schoolwork immeasurably. The following activities are designed to reinforce lessons already taught in the classroom. Before we begin, however, let's dress appropriately. How? By wearing our homework hats, of course!

All children know that once you put on your "HH" (otherwise known as a "Homework Hat"), your mind really starts to work actively, sharply, and creatively! Let the homework hat serve as a powerful reminder to children of their power to think. Use it to help your children with tasks such as math. If your daughter is learning simple arithmetic, why not put one hat plus one hat on top of your head and have her count how many there are? If your son is learning about history, why not have him put on his Colonial cap and describe it?

Spelling

Sometimes when I'm walking my son to school in the morning, I'll make a silly face and spontaneously say to him, "Oh my gosh. Look up ahead! The red rooster is racing royally across the race track. Really, how ridiculous. If only we remembered our red radishes the ride would be more reasonable. . . ," making almost everything in the story begin with the letter *r*. When he realizes what I'm doing, he gets this huge smile across his face and he then participates in the story too. When I want to introduce a different character, I'll use a different letter. For example, "Now look! A nutty newspaper is noisily nagging a nice newsboy. . . ," and so on. I never will warn him ahead of time or prepare him for our storytelling game. I think the spontaneity is much more fun and it lets my son know that creative thinking is part of the way we entertain ourselves.

ALICE O'DONNELL, mother of Emerson, 6, and Raymond, 2

I Miss You. Help your children learn the alphabet by trying the following storytelling game. Tell them, "Oh my gosh, there's bad news! The letter *Q* has disappeared. The police are out looking for him now. He just quit, ran away, gave up because he was so frustrated by his job. He hated the fact that he got used so rarely and then, only when the letter *U* was around. If *U* was busy somewhere else, he just sat around all day!!!! The only way he can come back is if people start saying words that have *Q* in them." Ask your child to come up with as many words as possible until *Q* finally returns. You can create similar stories with other letters of the alphabet too. You might suggest, for example, that your son won't be able to wear his baseball HAT because until *H* comes home, it's an 'AT. He also can't have any more hot dogs, Hershey bars, health food, or home fries unless they find *H* soon.

I wrote the following story many years ago, when I was working at a school where I observed a lot of intolerance on the part of students for those who were different or unusual. The story addresses prejudice, but will also strengthen your child's spelling skills at the same time.

And Sometimes Y

❋ Deep in the hills, nestled beneath tall oak trees, lies a small, neat, and complete community called Vowel Village. Naturally, it is inhabited by vowels, that's to say, *A, E, I, O, U,* and sometimes *Y*. I say sometimes *Y* because for some time *Y* lived there, and perhaps he might live there again, but for now, he is a wanderer and it is his story which I will share with you.

Vowel Village is very small. So small you have to use a magnifying glass to see it on the map. It only has five inhabitants, a close community, and it is for this reason that the villagers were nervous the first day *Y* drove into town.

Y had been living in Consonant Corners, a larger community of twenty-one residents on the other side of the mountain. But he was uneasy there. The *B*'s and *D*'s resonated harsh tones, he wasn't accepted by the more popular *R*'s, *T*'s, and *S*'s, and he had only gotten together once or twice with *X, Z,* and *Q*. He had often lain awake at night, listening to the gentle "ooooooohs," "aaaaaahs," and "uhuhuhuhs" that resonated throughout Vowel Village and over the mountain into Consonant Corner. He dreamed of a better life, where spirits were high and rents were low. So one day, he packed all his worldly goods and headed for the community over the mountain.

But when *Y* arrived, the villagers were not very nice, not very nice at all. They told him to go back where he had come from. They didn't want any of his harsh tones or aggressive spelling techniques. "Go home," they said, "go home and don't disturb the serenity of Vowel Village." *Y*, however, was determined, and explained that he was, indeed, half-vowel, and he would surely not disturb the tranquillity of the village. "I can be silent, really I can!" he exclaimed and recited *Aye* and *Eye*, *Oyster*, and *Allayed*. "Or, just stick me on the end of your words, like *Airy*, *Every*, *Olfactory*, *Unruly*, or *Inimitably*. The vowels were intrigued by *Y*'s logic and voted him in.

Y took his place at the end of words, happily adding the slightest alterations in sound, an extra syllable here and there, but always remaining subtle, and soft, amidst the placid vowels. And *Y* was ever so happy, and the vowels were ever so delighted, and they all lived in phonetic harmony. Until one day, something quite unexpected happened.

Y was attending a party given by *A* and *E*. There was a delectable assortment of pastries and gourmet helpings that *Y* munched and crunched on contentedly. Suddenly, quite unexpectedly, *Y* exclaimed, *"Your yams are yummy!"*

"*E*xcuse me?" said *E*.

"Your Yams are yummy! Yummy. Yummy. Yummy!" said *Y*, with total abandon.

"*A*wful!" shouted *A*.

"*U*nthinkable!" exclaimed *U*.

"*I*sn't *i*t *i*rritating?" mused *I*.

"*O*stentatious and *o*verbearing!" remarked *O*.

You see, *Y*, without thinking, had placed himself at the front of the word. Now the vowels were not used to hearing that kind of tone, not in their village, and I must say, they were taken off guard. They might have ignored *Y*'s boldness had he gone back to the back. But he couldn't see the harm. After all, he was just being himself, and the vowels liked him and accepted him.

Y began to say things like *yardstick* and *Yosemite* and *yesterday* and, at a particularly unruly town meeting, *Y* actually said "*You're yacking*!" The village began to resonate more loudly; after all, consonants do have that effect, and now the everpresent "ehs" and "ahs" blended with a new more distinct "Yo!"

"*E*nough!" said *E*.

"*O*ut of line and *o*ut of character," said *O*.

"*I*'m *a*fraid *Y* *i*s *u*nwelcome *i*n *o*ur *a*rea," they all concluded, and went to tell *Y* the unfortunate news.

"You're asking me to leave your area?" *Y* asked, stunned.

"It's our area now. No more *Y* to turn *our* into *your*, to make *am* into *yam* and *east* into *yeast,*" they told him.

Y sadly went home and packed his bags. He was in tears as he drove up the mountain road and out of Vowel Village.

The villagers were relieved to see him go. They went back to their comfortable routine, their "ooooohing" and "ahhhhhing," *e*ndeavors, and *u*ndertakings. And all was fine and all was well and the vowels were happy, if only for a little while.

You see, *Y* had made an impression on them. He had affected their lives, reordered their structures, given their words new meanings. The *E*'s missed their *eyes*, the *A*'s yearned for *anything*, the *O*'s longed for the *ordinary*, and *U*'s loss was *understandably* big.

That all happened some time ago and *Y* has still not returned. He's not staying at the *Y*. He didn't go back to Consonant Corners either; *E* checked and he was nowhere to be found. So if, on some clear, crisp night you should hear the *yearning* and the *yellings* of a sometimes *Y*, do tell him he's needed and wanted in Vowel Village. ❁

Math

Remember the story game we used to reinforce spelling, the one in which *Q* runs away? You can use this same technique to reinforce all sorts of other school subjects. Suppose your daughter is learning beginning math. Tell her that her teacher just called your house. Apparently the number *4* jumped off the blackboard that afternoon and ran out of the school building. The last time anyone saw *4*, it was heading in the direction of your home! She wants you to keep your eyes open for a wandering *4*. It has created quite a problem with all the four-year-olds in the neighborhood. Whenever someone asks them how old they are, they now have to change their answer to "I'm three plus one" or another equation that adds up to four. What are they? Let your child come up with a few more combinations. Then create an ending to the story. By simply personifying an object within the context of your child's homework, you can turn anything into a story.

History

You can enhance lessons on early American history by announcing to your child that one of the metal buttons on George Washington's pants has deserted. Exhausted from the Revolutionary War, the button decided to run. You can weave in a history lesson by explaining that zippers didn't exist in Colonial times, nor did Velcro or snaps. Buttons, made of metal, wood, or on the rare occasion, ivory, were the fastener of choice. Because of his disobedient button, George Washington almost lost his pants! He's now forced to hold them up with both his hands. The problem is, he needs one hand to carry his musket (here's your chance to explain what a musket, or early gun, was). Even if his button eventually returns, he won't be able to punish it properly, like the other soldiers who desert (here's your chance to talk about the seriousness of desertion during the war) because he needs to wear his pants again. In the meantime, perhaps Betsy Ross (here's your chance to discuss the designer of the American flag) can stitch a new pair of patriotic pants for him or, at the very least, sew a new button on his pants.

Geography

Do the same thing with geography. If New Jersey picked up and moved elsewhere, what would happen to the neighboring states? Wouldn't Pennsylvanians suddenly have oceanfront property? Wouldn't New Yorkers suddenly be forced to take a ferry boat to get off the island of Manhattan? Choose any state in the country and have it run away. Tell the story that ensues as a result.

Science

ASTRONOMY

If your daughter is studying astronomy, tell her that one of the stars from the Big Dipper left his spot in the constellation so that he could become a shooting star. He was jealous of all of those stars flying by so freely, while he had to stay in one place for billions of years. He had gotten bored and restless so he took off. Ask your child to draw the Big Dipper now that one of its stars is gone. What does she think the other stars in the Big Dipper should do? Should they hire another star or look for the one that left? Perhaps it joined another constellation like Orion. If so, what would Orion now look like? Illustrate the new constellation and finish the story.

I don't have the patience to make up long stories with my kids. Instead, I do snippets. I was trying to explain the three states of matter—solid, liquid, and gas—to my daughter. So I said, "See that cloud up there. It's filled with *gas*. If you were to stand on it, you'd fall right through. Of course, not everyone would fall through it. There are people who live on clouds. Angels and cherubs with wings. They cook up there and have dinner parties. When it rains, it's because they turn on the faucet or flush the toilet." My daughter thought that was the funniest thing.

STEVEN BLUM, father of Lilly, 5

RECYCLING AND THE ENVIRONMENT

I'll never forget the afternoon I performed at a public school in Brooklyn. My show was a musical storytelling extravaganza that taught kids to cherish the environment and have respect for nature. After the performance, the principal of the school stood in front of the auditorium and said, "Well boys and girls, we learned a lot today, didn't we?" "Yes!" they shouted in unison. "We learned to have respect for plants and flowers by not pulling them out of the ground or stomping on them, didn't we?" "Yes!" they shouted again. "And we learned to respect animals and all living creatures by not killing them—." Just then, a mosquito flew across his face. Spontaneously, he cupped his hands and SLAM!, squashed it dead. Silence pervaded the room for several seconds before I burst into laughter. "Oops, " he said, looking at me. "I guess I shouldn't have done that, huh?"

Many times the lessons we learn intellectually don't register unless we learn them emotionally as well. If a child empathizes rather than sympathizes with an object in nature, he's more likely to remember it by becoming emotionally connected to it. One of the best ways to achieve that "empathic" state is through the use of inanimate objects in storytelling. If your child is asked to portray a discarded soda can in a lonely, smelly landfill, chances are the next time he drinks a soda, he'll remember to recycle the can or return it for deposit, rather than throw his empty container in the trash can.

Reusable Usables. Pretend you're sitting next to a pile of discarded junk. Pick up each item and find new uses for it. For example, you might say to your kids, "Look at this huge refrigerator box some-one just threw out. What a shame! I bet they could have created something else with this. Can you tell me what you might have done with this box instead of throwing it out?" Take turns finding new uses for other items including an old television antenna, an empty coffee can, and an old television.

Landfill Blues. Ask your child to become an object in a landfill. Perhaps he's a discarded old wooden shingle, a piece of copper tubing, or a plastic Hula-Hoop, which takes thousands of years to fully disintegrate into the earth. Discuss decomposition and how long different objects take to work their way back into the soil. What does it feel like to live in the dump? What was their life like before they were thrown away? Is there anything they can do to get back to the way they were? Create a story surrounding the adventures of that object.

Look for the Recycling Symbol. One of the easy ways you can peak your child's interest in recycling is to show her the recycling symbol that exists on many packages right inside your home. Tell your child that each item that displays this symbol was produced from recycled materials, thereby protecting our environment by reducing the amount of trash we create. Here's a story I wrote to help children recognize the merits of recycling newspapers and old boxes.

The Magic Map

❅ There once was a woman named Mrs. Popsicle, because she was tall and skinny like a popsicle stick. She had bright yellow hair and wore a funny purple hat. Mrs. Popsicle was very organized, neat, and tidy. Her favorite pastime was dusting underneath the refrigerator and behind the oven.

One day, she came home from the grocery store with an armful of groceries and, naturally, put them away immediately, singing as she sorted.

"Oh, the ice cream in the freezer,
The soap goes on the sink,
The cereal in the cabinet,
In the fridge there's plenty to drink

Oh, the pots go on the counter.
The pans go on the shelf.
The cookies are on the table,
To those just help yourself."

And when she had finished she went upstairs to practice the violin. This meant the kitchen was empty. Plenty of time for the boxes in the cabinet to get to know each other. There was Barry Bran Flakes, Charlie Cornflake, Sugar Frosted Sally, and Easy Bake Brenda. And they all became the best of friends, laughing, giggling, and guffawing whenever they were out of earshot of Mrs. Popsicle.

One day, a new box came into the cupboard. It was sporting an orange bow tie and was shiny. His name was Peter Pasta, and within a matter of hours, Peter Pasta and Charlie Cornflake were buddies.

The next day Charlie put his arm around Peter's shoulder and said, "Peter, if we ever get separated, use this map, and you'll find me." It was an unusual map, with three arrows going round and round in a circle. But before Peter had time to put it in his pocket, the door to the cabinet swung open and the map fell to the floor. A long skinny hand reached inside and grabbed Peter by the waist. He was about to be eaten! The next thing he knew, his top was popped, his spinach noodles were emptied into a pot, and he was crumpled and thrown into the garbage bag. And because Mrs. Popsicle was so organized and tidy, she immediately took the trash with Peter in it and deposited him in the pail outside for the garbage man to pick up.

Peter was frantic. "I've got to get out of here! I'll wind up crushed, pounded, or squashed. I'll be burned in an incinerator or spend the rest of my days in a smelly landfill."

He tried to pull himself to the top of the garbage can. But no sooner did he rise to the top of the pail when he slid over its steep sides and rolled down the long hill in front of Mrs. Popsicle's house. "Charlie will help me! I've got to find my way back to him!" he said, and started to climb up the steep hill, inch by inch. Suddenly, a bicycle came zooming down the hill and flattened his head like a pancake. But he lifted himself up and started to climb up the hill again. He was halfway up the hill when seventeen joggers, training for the New York Marathon, pounded over his already bruised box top. "Ugh, yikes, ouch, oy!" By the time he made it up the hill to Mrs. Popsicle's house, he looked crumpled, filthy, and ragged, like . . . well, like a piece of garbage!

He was so flat he was able to slide under Mrs. Popsicle's front door. As soon as he entered the house, he tiptoed into the kitchen, opened the pantry door . . . and Charlie was gone! Vanished! He'd been eaten! "What should I do now?" Peter asked in a panic. And that's when Peter's eyes fell on the magic map on the floor. He remembered Charlie's words: "If we ever get separated, use this map, and you'll find me."

He picked it up off the floor and followed the arrows, around and around and around and around and around and around and splat!!! He smacked face first into the cabinet. "Ouch!!!! This map is useless!!! Bah ha bah ha. Boo hoo hoo Waaaa waaa waaaa." He wailed like a baby. He could hardly see through his tears as he slid under the front door and sat on the outside stoop, sobbing.

Unbeknownst to Peter, a miracle was looming. At that very moment, a huge gust of wind arrived. It picked up Peter and carried him over houses and red cars and shopping malls and office buildings, past church steeples and lush hills and parking lots and drive-in movie theaters, and dropped him—Ouch!—right atop a bicycle, parked in front of a grocery store. He looked through the glass window and there it was! The Magic Map, sitting on the belly of a box of cornflakes. Not just any cornflakes. It was Charlie Cornflake! Peter ran inside and hugged Charlie and said, "Hey, how did you end up here, all shiny and new?"

And Charlie explained to his buddy that the map was really a special recycling symbol. "Every time you see one of these maps on our bellies, it means we've been recycled from old paper and cardboard and made new again."

"Hey, I'd like to be shiny and new too!" said Peter, and he threw himself into the recycling bin at the front of the store. "See you soon Charlie!" he said as he landed atop a pile of old newspapers. So the next time you're in the grocery store, look for the Magic Map. It may even be Peter Pasta. ❈

Flower Power. Ask your children to take turns pretending to plant various flowers, plants, or trees. Have family members guess what they've planted. Make sure they act out specific features of the object, like height, width, weight, smell of its flowers, and the prick of its needles. For example, if the object your daughter plants is a rose, make sure she pretends to smell it and touch it and— OUCH!—watch out for those thorns. If your son selected an apple tree, make sure that he plucks and eats at least one apple from its branches.

More Flower Power. Choose a flower, plant, or tree and start talking about your life as that object. Don't actually say what you are. Let other family members guess, based on your personal story. For example, if you are a lilac bush, you might say, "People are jealous of me because I'm so beautiful. What can I say? They're right. I'm always dressed in the most up-to-date purple clothes, I wear fabulous perfume that people come for miles to smell, and I'm popular too. Bees swarm around me."

Nature Sounds. Go outside and close your eyes. Raise a finger each time you hear a different sound in nature. If you're not a country kid, you'll be amazed at how hard this activity is. This activity will help children become more attuned to nature.

Squirrel Talk. Choose a popular story with which you're familiar. Take turns telling that story in the language of an animal. If you're a dog, you must bark the entire story. If you're a cat, meow your tale. You'll need to rely on other storytelling devices besides vocabulary, such as hand and body movement, facial expressions, and voice modulation.

2

"When I Was a Kid, I Walked Twelve Miles to School in the Snow"

How to Collect and Share Your Family's Folklore

> *To be a person is to have a story to tell.*
> ISAK ÐINESEN

On an ordinary afternoon in 1967, I came home crying, "Mrs. Ross is the meanest teacher I've ever had!" My father, a street-mart Brooklynite with a chronic twinkle in his eye, knew the perfect antidote for my grammar school woes. "You think your teacher is mean?" he said. "You don't know what mean is until you've experienced Miss Moldy."

He proceeded to describe his third-grade schoolmarm, a 1930s disciplinarian with wire-rim glasses and a black dress buttoned to her chin, whose merciless gaze and "spanking stick" inspired even the naughtiest students to tow the line. Apparently, one day my father arrived late to school. Miss Moldy, a stickler for tardiness, made him bend over and was about to spank him in front of his classmates when fate intervened. A fire drill happened at that very moment, and in the chaos, my father escaped his public flogging.

I was mesmerized by my dad's anecdote. Suddenly, my own situation with nasty Mrs. Ross didn't seem so bad after all. In sharing his story with me, my father not only put things into perspective, but also comforted me by reminding me of our common experience. Instinctively, he understood that in revealing his personal story he not only would be showing me a hidden side of himself, but also would be schooling me in some of life's lessons.

How I loved to hear his stories, particularly about his neighborhood in Brooklyn. There were the wild adventures in the Botanic Garden with his twin sister, Evelyn, the romps through the Egyptian mummy exhibit at the Brooklyn Museum, and a medley of memorable characters, like Patrick, the warmhearted Irish cop who would cheerily guide my father and his school chums across the street each day . . . until one day, he was arrested for running a bookie operation on President Street.

My mother was a different type of storyteller altogether. Unlike my father, her storehouse of personal anecdotes had a lock on it that no one, not even her irrepressible daughter, could break. Taken away to a concentration camp by the Nazis as a young girl, she learned to survive by stitching up all her painful memories into a tightly bound quilt. Instinctively, I knew at a young age that if any part of the stitching came undone, her whole quilt would come unraveled. Yet even though my mother never spoke of her past, her story tumbled out inadvertently. It was in her face, hollowed and frightened all the time, and in her tears, which would fall for no reason, during a Little League game or a family outing, when she should have been laughing. Her story revealed itself each year on the holidays, like Yom Kippur, when the piano in the corner of the dining room was covered with so many memorial candles, one for every member of her family who died in the camps, that the glow was blinding, or on Chanukah, when she would place a menorah in the window, alit with a rainbow of luminous candles, then pull the shades down. Despite her best efforts to shield us from her dark past, her silence told a story, nonetheless. I'm convinced that I became a professional storyteller as a way of mending all of those broken stories.

All of us need to tell and hear our family's stories. Without them, we're like trees trying to grow with severed roots. We must know where we've come from in order to know where we're going.

Dark and light, family stories are as essential as breathing. To think of them as something superfluous is to deny one of our most basic instincts—to communicate. Family stories help us determine who we are in the world and how we fit in. They nurture us and guide us through life, showing us how to mourn and celebrate, how to live and how to die. Though not always factually accurate, they reveal an awful lot about a family member's hopes, fears, and dreams. They provide us with a strong sense of right and wrong and convey guiding principles and morals to children. They are also one of the best ways to get close to your kids. By revealing your past, you're allowing your children to know you as a full person.

Parents who attend my storytelling workshops tell me they'd like to tell more personal stories but don't feel they have a good story to tell. Part of the reason we've become intimidated about sharing our stories is that we place so much attention on the *finished product* and not on the *process* of recalling. Reaching into your memory bank shouldn't have to result in a movie-of-the-week. That kind of pressure would make anyone clam up. Anyway, it's the minutiae that are really fascinating, especially to your children.

When I look back on my own childhood, I realize that while my mother was unwilling to share the biggest story of her life with me—her wartime experiences—my saving grace was that she overflowed with the small stories that make up the details of everyday life.

> Cultivate the margins.
>
> QUENTON ANDERSON

I can recall the countless hours she spent with her sisters (the Gabor sisters of New Jersey) in our living room. Roszika, Borishka, and my mother, Sarika, would sit around our kitchen table gossiping intently about absolutely nothing. They would create a story out of the most ridiculous piece of information, a sale at Kmart or our neighbors' plastic surgery. (Apparently, one afternoon, the mother and two daughters from next door got nose jobs and all arrived home together with Band-Aids on their noses.) They would turn small incidents into world-class events, discussing everything in detail as if their lives depended on it. They would lean in toward the teller, resolutely listening, their eyes bulging with excitement.

While their love of gossip may not have been the most admirable trait to pass down to me, their love of story was. They approached small details with the enthusiasm of a child. Whether they knew it or not, their ability to elevate the mundane is a quality that makes for the finest stories.

> The maturity of man is reacquiring the seriousness that one had as a child at play.
>
> FRIEDRICH NIETZSCHE

Don't try to be fascinating. You don't have to tell complex, fully developed stories. A simple memory is enough! Start with the color of your first book bag, the smell of your childhood kitchen on weekends, the sound of the Good Humor truck as it rode into your neighborhood. Don't underestimate the joy your kids will have when you recall for them these small memories.

But even if you have a strong desire to collect and share your family's rich folklore, where do you begin? Through the years I've developed some guidelines that can be adapted to your own needs and circumstances. They are divided into age-appropriate activities. Some require equipment, like tape recorders and cameras. Others rely only on the imaginations and memories of the participants. Whatever the activity, don't feel compelled to reveal a sensationalistic story to entertain your children. Even the simplest family anecdote will bedazzle and delight them.

THE WORLD OF CHILDHOOD

When we played baseball we used a broom handle and a rubber ball.
A manhole cover was first base, second base was a lamppost, and Mr.
Gitletz, who used to bring a kitchen chair down to watch us play,
was third base. One time I slid into Mr. Gitletz.
He caught the ball and tagged me out.
GEORGE BURNS

Memory Maps

Memories of play can be the best vehicle for tapping into memory. That's because play is the most serious endeavor to a child, and the most universally joyous.

Map One: Play Time
MATERIALS: *Paper and pencil*
Draw a map of your favorite spot where you played as a child and share with your children a particular story that happened at that site. Once your children are familiar with the activity, have them ask other family members to do the same. As a follow-up activity, encourage your children to keep a scrapbook of these play maps along with their accompanying stories. Make sure they mark which family member belongs to each map.

Every other house on my block in Cleveland had a relative living in it. As a kid it was wonderful because everyone knew you. On Saturdays, when everyone was out walking, you couldn't go four feet without seeing a cousin, an aunt, a grandparent. Everyone would stop you and pinch your cheeks. It took an hour to get down the block.

LEON SPERO

Map Two: Your Block

MATERIALS: *Paper and pencil*

Draw the block you grew up on and describe it to your child. Make sure to include as many details as you can remember, including everything from where the fire hydrant was to where the tallest tree (if any) on your block was. Encourage your child to ask you questions about that block. If you like, you can start with the following questions:

Were there other kids nearby?

If so, who were they and where did they live in relation to you?

Was there a bully on the block?

How about a practical joker?

Where did they live?

Can you remember an incident that happened with them?

Where was the post office?

How about your school?

Where did you do your grocery shopping?

Map Three: Ridin' in My Car

MATERIALS: *Pencil and paper*

Draw a map of the first car you remember riding in as a child. Describe a memorable incident that happened in that car. Here are some possible questions:

Who usually drove the car, grandma or grandpa?

Did you wear seatbelts then?

Did your cars drive as fast as ours do?

Did you go on road trips? Where to?

Who joined you on those trips?

Which was the most fun trip and why?

Have them do the same with other relatives.

House Tour. Close your eyes and travel back to your childhood home. Keeping your eyes closed, walk in the front door and open the first door you see in your mind. Enter the room and tell your kids everything you see. Now take a whiff and describe everything that you smell. Touch an object in that room and describe its texture. What can you hear? Music? Silence? People chatting in another room? Share any sounds you hear with your kids. Leave that room and enter another. Do the same thing with several rooms in your apartment or house. If your kids interrupt you during the middle of your recollections with a question, simply keep your eyes shut and try to answer them. When you've finished traveling throughout your childhood home, open the front door and exit. Then open your eyes and watch the look of fascination on the faces of your kids.

Can I Lick the Bowl? Tastes have a way of staying with us, long after we've eaten. Close your eyes and travel back to your childhood kitchen. Visualize your mother or father reaching toward you with a spoon, filled with something edible. Taste it and describe its flavor. Is it chocolate cake batter? Medicine? Is your mother asking you to sample the soup she's about to serve for dinner? Now try the same activity in the kitchen of your grandparent's home. Repeat the same activity substituting other serving utensils like silver tongs or a wooden spoon.

The First Time. "Firsts" are always memorable and can be the best way for tapping into your relatives' stories. Ask them to describe their first

1. Bicycle
2. Kiss
3. Trip away from home
4. Fancy party
5. Car
6. House
7. Pet
8. Teacher
9. Job
10. Camping trip

Make up other firsts too and add them to your list.

As Time Goes By. Pick up a paper clock at any stationery supply store, the kind you hang on your door to let people know when you'll be back in your office. Together with your kids, choose one or two key periods from your childhood, for example, high school days or summer camp. Ask your kids to move the hands of the clock to a time of their choosing, say 3 o'clock. Describe where you usually were at 3 o'clock during that childhood period. Have your kids change the times on the clock and respond accordingly.

This Is Your Life. Ask your child to be the host of a talk show in which you are the guest. But instead of playing yourself, become a person from your past. Perhaps you're that strict grammar school principal you dreaded. Or maybe the friendly mail carrier who always patted you on the head as he walked by. Have your child ask you questions about your life. Involve other family members by making them audience members who may have questions to ask. Reverse roles. Have your child become a character from his past and you become the host.

If you want to really make this activity fun, instead of a person, become a historical object, such as an old quilt passed down from your grandmother. As that quilt, become a guest and talk about your life. Have your kids do the same. Even if your kids don't get all the historical facts completely accurate, they will have fun with a general period of history and will gain new knowledge along the way.

Coat of Many Colors. Pantomime putting on an imaginary coat, the kind you used to wear throughout your adolescence. Act out its general shape, weight, and style for your children and have them guess what type of coat it is. Perhaps it's your first lettered jacket. Maybe it's your brand new Easter Sunday coat or the raincoat your mother used to make you wear on stormy days. Once your kids have tried guessing, describe the coat in as much detail as possible. (You can also draw it, if you like.) Add any memories or stories associated with each coat.

Growth Chat. Add a thin strip of paper, vertically, alongside your child's growth chart. The next time you measure how tall your child has gotten, ask her to add a short paragraph next to her size marking, describing an interesting thing that happened that day or a simple activity she participated in. Over time, you'll be able to measure the changes in her life story as well as her height.

Story Cookbook. *You'll need index cards and an index card box for this activity.* Behind every recipe lies a story. Sometimes notes will be attached to recipes like, "This is Dad's favorite," or "This is the one Aunt Shirley always makes for Thanksgiving." Create your own story cookbook by combining family recipes with accompanying stories. Here's how it works: Go through an old recipe box with your children. When you come to a recipe that has a memory attached to it, copy that recipe onto a blank index card. Then try to remember the details of the story behind the recipe and write it down next to the recipe. Who gave you that particular recipe? What was the occasion? Did you taste a great dessert at someone's Christmas party and ask the host for the recipe? If so, where was the party? Who attended? Describe the surroundings and any guests who may have been there. Write down the details of when and where you might have eaten the food. Describe the smells, sights, and sounds in the room at the time. When you are done, insert the recipe/story index cards into your new index card box. Encourage your kids to add recipe/story cards to the box whenever they can.

WHAT'S IN A NAME?

> At that time, everybody had nicknames. Take my old gang. There was Moose. He looked like a moose. Bagels, Shy, Tippi, and me they called Legs, cause I had a nice pair of legs. My brother who was very skinny they called Schmaltz, which means fat in Yiddish. My other brother, who was never in a hurry, they called him Jeep. My kid brother, they called him Gangy. He used to talk like a tough guy. If somebody came around and asked for Joe or Pete or Willy, we'd say, "Who?"
>
> BLANCHE LASKY,
> from *You Must Remember This* by Jeff Kisseloff

The small grocery store in my neighborhood still sells penny candies. Now, I have a passion for caramels, and when I spotted a container of them on the counter one day, I knew I was in big trouble, knowing that if I didn't control myself, I would devour the entire contents in an hour. I made a pact: I would allow myself one caramel a day. The owners of the shop, three Yemenite brothers, found my daily one-caramel habit to be very amusing. So one day, one of the brothers started calling me "Caramel." And the name stuck. Now, a year later, if one of the brothers sees me on the street he'll call out, "Caramel!" And I love it. I love the sense of community and continuity it gives me, and the feeling that I'm noticed in an era of hustle and bustle, when it's easy to feel anonymous.

Our names are like doors to our lives. Behind each one is a story. Sometimes our last names reveal the trades that our forefathers once had, like "Smith" (for a blacksmith or gold or silver smith) or "Schumaker" (shoe maker), or the cities or regions they came from. Other times, names memorialize people who have died or honor those who are still alive. Often, names represent the hopes, dreams, yearnings, or passions of those who named us.

Name Game. Share the story behind your name with your children. You can use your first, last, or middle name. If you have a nickname, confirmation name, or Hebrew name, you can use those too. Have your children share a story about their names as well. Perhaps they can recall a naming incident as a child. For example, their little sister may have had a hard time pronouncing a name and may have substituted another word in its place. This is also a wonderful activity to do with older relatives during family get-togethers.

I think it's important for kids to know about their family history and where they came from, to have a sense of continuity. One of the ways I give that to them is through this simple little story that I tell them just before bedtime. Since my kids are only three and five, I keep the story extremely basic with very few details so it makes it easier for the girls to focus on how their lineage works. I say, "There once was little girl named Holly (my name) who lived with her parents named Ginny and Andy (my parents' names). They lived in New Jersey in a lovely white wooden house with a cherry tree in the front yard. When the little girl grew up, she moved to New York City. At the same time there was also a little boy named Steven (my husband's name) who lived with his parents named Rosemary and Joe (his parents' names). He lived in an apartment in New York. Holly moved to Manhattan and met Steven and they fell in love. After they got married, they decided they had so much love, they wanted to share it with another person and so they had a baby named Lilly (my older daughter), and they loved her so much they wanted her to have a friend. So they had another baby named April (my younger daughter). . . ." It seems like the dumbest little tale but they keep asking for it over and over again.

HOLLY KLEIN, mother of Lilly, 5, and April, 3

THE STUFF OF OUR LIVES

Family objects are stories waiting to emerge. Yet an object doesn't have to be an antique or expensive artifact in order to have historical significance. A simple rag doll, passed down from generation to generation, can tell as much about a family's history as a priceless antique. The key is to see the story in everything. Even the folding chair you picked up last summer at Wal-Mart has stories to tell. Didn't you bring it to the beach or lounge on it in your backyard? If so, that chair has become part of your family's lore. If it could talk, it would surely have gossip to share about the conversations that happened in its presence, the people who sat in it, the food that was served.

Remember, to a child, all toys and objects are alive. (On some level, I still think my childhood Raggedy Andy doll has conversations in my absence.) Use that sense of personification in the objects you deal with. Don't worry too much about dates and times, or about being 100 percent factually accurate. If your children have a positive experience with a family artifact, they will yearn to explore that object in more detail when they get older. For now, your job is to mine that object for its rich stories, a task that will leave your children with a sense of wonder and delight.

The following activities will help jog memories while providing your children with clues to their rich and varied pasts.

If This Object Could Talk. Gather a variety of different objects, both old and new, from around the house. Have your children pose the following question to different members of your family: If this object could talk, what stories would it have to tell? At what occasions has it been present? Who used it, touched it, damaged it, repaired it, or played with it? How did you get it? Was it a gift? A purchase? Do you enjoy it? Did it belong to anyone else and, if so, who?

The Key Game. Pull a ring of keys from your pocket after dinner. Choose one key and describe an adventure or a funny thing that happened inside the room it opens. Perhaps the key to the attic reminds you of a diary you store there, filled with childhood memories. Find another key to a different room and tell the story it evokes. Have other family members do the same with their keys. Even the simplest stories and memories can fascinate your children.

Word Game. Throw out the name of an object, any object. Take turns sharing any personal story, memory, or anecdote inspired by that object. For example, the word *diamond* might make you recall the time you proposed to your wife, or the time you went shopping with your husband for your ring. Have your children call out the name of objects, too. Remember: *Everyone* has a story to tell, no matter how silly or insignificant it might seem at first.

THE HEALING PLACE: HOSPITAL STORIES

When my father was in his 80s, he suffered a heart attack. Now, he was a religious Jew from the old country, Poland. And although he lived in the Bronx, he still practiced his religion, spoke Yiddish, went to synagogue regularly, the whole thing. Anyway, when I came home from work one night, I got word that my father had been taken to a Catholic hospital near his apartment. I jumped in a cab and went to see him right away. And when I got to his room, I see him surrounded by Sisters in habits, and hanging over his bed there's a wooden statue of Jesus. I say, "Dad, are you okay with the fact that Jesus is hanging over your head?" Without missing a beat he says, "It couldn't hurt."

R. PERRY

We all knew my cousin's wife, Linda, was level-headed. Still, nothing proved that fact more definitively than the tale she spun for us over dinner recently.

Apparently, months before her delivery date, she began preparing the nursery for her new baby. The walls had already been painted a beautiful dusty rose. The new wooden crib and changing table had claimed their places under the large window at the far end of the room. And the plush, red carpet was scheduled for installation weeks before the baby's expected arrival.

Unfortunately, the carpet men never arrived on the day they said they would. Nor did they the day after that, or the day after that. Finally, Linda, fuming, called the carpet store, and the owner promised to handle the matter immediately. She hung up the phone and waited. And waited. And waited some more.

Five days later, Linda went into labor. "Honey, it's time!" she shouted to my cousin Robert, as she gathered up her nightie and toothbrush and made her way to the car. Robert ran back into the house to grab some last-minute provisions, when suddenly the doorbell rang. It was the carpet delivery man, ready to install their order. Robert was flustered. "Ugh . . . gee . . . I don't know . . . I can't . . . You see. . . ." But Linda sprang—or should I say, waddled—into action. "You have to stay, honey," she calmly told my cousin. "If you turn these guys away now, they're never going to come back." "But honey—" "It's okay, dear. I won't give birth for a while," she said. " I'll take myself to the hospital. You'll meet me there after the carpet is laid." She calmly climbed into her car and sped down the road toward the hospital while the men rolled out the red carpet in preparation for her return.

Believe it or not, one of the best ways to elicit stories from people, particularly from the elderly, is through hospital stories. Remember, not all hospital stories are sad. The birth of a child, for example, is a joyous occasion and a story many family members are happy to share. So is healing after an illness. Although we're not used to asking our older relatives to recount such memories, many people actually want to share their hospital stories. Telling them to a generation once removed, such as a grandchild or grand niece or nephew, can make the retelling easier emotionally and can bring out some powerful and important memories.

Have your children ask a relative about his or her hospital stay. You and your kids will be amazed at how freely the stories will fall.

RED AS A BEET: EMBARRASSING STORIES

My mother loves to shop at Labels for Less. Everyone who works at that store knows her, and when there's a sale, they phone her and tell her about it. Well, one afternoon she gets a call from one of the salesgirls who tells her that an item my mother bought a few hours earlier just went on sale. "If you can bring in the item with the receipt, we'll credit you for the difference," she says. My mother knew exactly which trash can she had thrown the receipt in earlier that day—it was the one on the end of her block. So she quickly runs out her door in her bath slippers and an old plaid housecoat, wearing an old ratty wig with a scarf over it. She figured she would grab the receipt and go back inside. But as she bends over the trash can and starts fishing for the receipt, an elegantly dressed man in an Armani suit taps my mother on the shoulder and hands her a five-dollar bill. "I really want you to have this," he says. "No, you don't understand," she says, trying to explain her situation to him. "I understand perfectly," he says, adding, "This is no time to be proud." Well, my mom looked down at her outfit and realized he was right!

LOIS B.

Maybe it was the time I held my mother's hand in the packed elevator of a department store, only to find out, when the door opened, that I'd been clutching a strange man's palm. Or maybe it was the time Emile de Becque's mustache came off on my face, during a staged kiss, in the third act of *South Pacific,* in front of a packed high school auditorium.

There have been so many embarrassing moments in my life that it's hard to award first prize to any one of them. If there's one universal feature that binds mankind it's this: Everyone has an embarrassing story and no one ever forgets it. Ask a relative to recall his or her most embarrassing moment. You may be surprised by the outcome.

THERE'S A FLY IN YOUR SOUP:
PRACTICAL JOKE STORIES

My cousin Gigi and I had been patiently sitting with my mother in the motor vehicles office for over an hour, waiting for her driver's license to be renewed. We were only ten years old, and we were tired and cranky. Gigi's leg started to fall asleep, so she carefully placed her foot at the very edge of the chair in front of her, so as not to disturb the woman who was sitting in it. Of course, I couldn't let an opportunity like that go by. I lightly tapped Gigi's foot, causing her to kick the woman right in the butt!

Ah, the joys of practical jokes, the delectable pleasure we get when temporarily torturing friends. Of course, we don't feel so great when the tables are reversed and we become the victim of practical jokes. Ask your family members to share a practical joke story. You'll be amazed to learn how mischievous certain family members once were.

NAUGHTY NAUGHTY: DISCIPLINE STORIES

All of my classmates used to smoke cigarettes before school. I wanted to be like the other kids so one morning, I stole my father's two remaining cigarettes from his cigarette case, which was lying on the kitchen table. When he reached for them and saw that they were gone, he asked everyone in my family, "Does anyone know where my cigarettes are?" We all shook our heads, and shortly thereafter, I headed off to school. When I got there, all the kids were standing outside smoking, and I reached into my pocket for the two cigarettes . . . and they were gone! I knew my father had found them and had removed them from my coat. But when I got home, he never mentioned the incident. I was mortified. I would have preferred it if he had hit me or something, but the fact that he never said anything— it was worse than any punishment. I felt totally disappointed in myself, and believe me, I never did anything like that again.

SARI B.

My parents brought me and my brother to a handful of parades when we were young. There was the Veterans Day parade in Weehawken, New Jersey, where our plumber lived; the Fourth of July parade on Martha's Vineyard, where we vacationed one summer; and the Rose Bowl parade, which cousin Renata brought us to when we visited her in Pasadena. They were exciting events, no doubt, yet my memory of them pales in comparison to the afternoon my parents canceled our trip to the Macy's Thanksgiving Day parade in New York City.

All month long, I had been looking forward to that parade. But on the morning of the event, my brother and I got into a minor squabble. "If you two don't stop fighting, we're not going to the parade!" my father said. And sure enough, he kept his word. I can still feel the overwhelming disappointment at missing that parade, an acute pain that lodged in the pit of my stomach for days.

Stories about discipline, though not always pleasant, reveal an awful lot about family dynamics, character traits, and values. Take turns sharing one. Remember to include the clever ways you may have escaped punishment, or your memory of the strictest disciplinarian in your school. This is an activity in which young children will be able to share, as well as collect, stories.

PHOTOGRAPHS

> Through photography, each family constructs a portrait of itself, a kit of images that bears witness to its connectedness.
> SUSAN SONTAG, *On Photography*

Picture This. Get out your box of old photographs—preferably those that were taken before your kids were born—and share the stories that accompany each picture. If other living relatives are included in the photos, have your children pay them a visit and bring the photographs. Have them pose the following questions:

When was this photo taken?

How old were you then?

Where were you?

Was it a vacation? If so, how did you decide on that place?

Were you married then? If not, who were you dating at the time?

What is your strongest memory of that event?

Do you still have the clothes you wore at the time of the picture? If not, what happened to them? What other kinds of clothes did you wear at that time?

Enhance this activity by making it more interactive. One of the best ways to engage your kids in an activity is by asking lots of questions. For example, you might want to hold the photograph up and ask your children, "What year do you think this was?" "What kinds of clothes do you think people wore then?" "Based on this photo, can you guess what people did in their spare time?"

Tape It! The next time you go on an outing with your children, bring along a hand-held microphone. Tape your random thoughts, songs, conversations, or jokes that you share during your day together. Your musings may seem mundane or insignificant to you at the time, but the tape will preserve family memories while becoming a source of delight to your young children (ages 3–5) when they listen to it later.

When my daughter was four, my father took her for a walk and brought along his small tape recorder. As they walked, he talked into the recorder, describing everything they were seeing along the way. "Look, we're coming up to the ducks! . . . Hey, there's a funny looking leaf. . . . Now we're coming home." At the end, you can hear the two of them singing together. It was the simplest idea, but my daughter absolutely loves that tape. She listens to it again and again. She's able to stay close to her grandpa even though he lives over a thousand miles away.

DEBORAH PARIS, mother of
Molly, 6, Jonah, 3, and Hannah, 11 days old

FAMILY EXPRESSIONS

Family expressions are the poetry of everyday life. If you think long enough, you'll be able to recall a turn of phrase or set of words that were used within the inner circle of your family. They are filled with meaning because of the stories they carry with them. Hearing a family expression, we can often remember the humorous or poignant moment that gave rise to its inception.

I remember when the first discount store opened up in my hometown, selling a bit of everything, from clothing to furniture. Back then, there were virtually no wholesale places open to the public, and when my mother and her sisters heard about the store, they rushed there in the hopes of finding a bargain. Although they came home with a storehouse of stuff, my mother still declared, "That place is a real junky." From then on, any time a new store opened, my family would ask, "Is it a junky?"

In *A Celebration of American Family Folklore* by Steve Zeitlin, Amy Kotkin, and Holly Cutting Baker, Margaret Clark says,

When I was young I bought my brother a book for his birthday, a biography of Houdini. He had barely unwrapped it when I grabbed it back from him and ran away and hid for the rest of the birthday party and read the book. It was a big joke that I had bought him a book which I obviously wanted. So ever after that, anytime anyone gave a gift that was clearly something that the giver wanted perhaps more than the givee, it was called a *Houdini.*

If you think about it long enough, you'll realize that your family also has its own unique expressions. What are they? Ask your children to help you recall the expressions used by various members of your family and write them down along with the stories that gave rise to them. The following can help you get started:

1. A family expression used around my house is _____.
2. The story that started it was _____.
3. Other family expressions I've heard at a cousin's, aunt's and uncle's, or grandparent's house are _____.
4. The stories that started them are _____.

FAMILY CUSTOMS

A tradition isn't only something that we receive.
It's also something that we create.

Phrase etched into a library window,
Amsterdam Avenue, New York City

Whether you realize it or not, if you've ever had a backyard barbecue on Memorial Day or called your dog with a particular sound, you've established a family custom. True, many people throw birthday parties for their children. But do they make a twelve-colored Jell-O mold cake in a giant glass bowl, as my mother did each year?

The shared activities we call customs are often unique to each family. Often, they begin with a story. For example, when my father was a little boy, milk would be delivered in glass bottles, straight from the dairy farms. Since milk wasn't homogenized back then, the cream would separate from the rest and float to the top of my father's cup. To mix it all up, he would have to shake his cup in a circular motion before drinking. The funny thing is, he still shakes his cup today—regardless of what he's drinking!

Many families enjoy the fact that they have certain traditions, even if they are practiced only on special occasions. For Antonio Amato, from Chicago, that meant celebrating Christmas with his family's own distinctive Italian flavoring:

> The biggest thing at Christmas is having our special antipasto on Christmas Eve. We'd go to mass and come back and have hard salami and a great homemade tomato soup. Food was the thing that brought everybody together. It wasn't so much a religious holiday as it was celebrating with family, the realization that we were still together, still healthy.

Family customs not only mark time, but also tell a wonderful story about the individual natures of families. Help your children recall some of your own customs by either writing or telling them.

1. Describe a family custom._____.
2. The story behind it is_____.
3. Other family customs I've experienced at a friend's or relative's house are_____.
4. The stories that started them are_____.

FAMILY CHARACTERS

Every family has at least one eccentric member, the one who wears outlandish hats, has strange habits, or is always saying embarrassing things. Ask the oldest members of your family, like grandparents or great uncles and aunts, to describe some of the family eccentrics who were around during their youth. If they can't come up with kin, ask them to describe a memorable family friend or business acquaintance.

I love the following story by professional storyteller Jackie Torrence, from her book *Jackie Tales,* in which she reminisces about her favorite aunt.

Aunt Sally and Uncle Fifth

❀ Now, when I was four years old, the person that stood out in my life, the one I liked best of all, was my aunt Sally. I *loved* Aunt Sally. Aunt Sally was a fat woman. I loved Aunt Sally 'cause she was golden brown all over. Her color was smooth, like hot chocolate with cream in it. And her skin was *soft*, it always had a little shine to it, as I remember. . . .

Well, I liked Aunt Sally because when she walked she had a little jiggle. I used to walk behind her and watch that and think about it.

"Wouldn't it be nice if I could jiggle like that?"

And so I used to say that to my grandmother.

"I want to jiggle like Aunt Sally," I said.

Now, to a woman like my grandmother, who was like my mother, 98 pounds, that was disgraceful.

"You know, Sally's got too much behind.

"And Sally's got too much in front too."

She always wore low-cut dresses. And so a lot of her popped out, you know, and I liked that too. I could just see myself with all of that jiggling up in front of me and behind me too.

And so I'd say, "I want to look like Aunt Sally."

My grandmother would look down at me.

"You'd better watch out what you ask God for," she said. "He may give it to you."

Well now, I was blessed with Aunt Sally's jiggle. And I had to deal with it because I asked for it. You know, my grandmother said, if I asked for it . . .

Aunt Sally smelled *goood.* I didn't know what it was, but when I'd go near her she smelled just like a pound cake. Now, you have not smelled *anything* until you have smelled the first odor of a pound cake baking in the oven. That's how Aunt Sally smelled.

And it makes your mouth water.

I don't care how old or how young you are, that first smell of that pound cake, if it's made right, it's gonna make you salivate.

Aunt Sally smelled like that all the time.

And I didn't know why.

Grandma said she used vanilla flavoring for perfume. To a four-year-old, what could that mean?

Well, one day Grandma was making a cake in a great big old bowl. . . .

Well, she was whipping that cake, you know, with these little bottles on the table. Course, I talked all the time, and so I asked her what *that* was, and what *that* was and *that* was, and she told me coconut flavoring, banana flavoring, walnut flavoring, and then she said, "*That's* vanilla flavoring."

Aaahaaaaah . . .

And so, when she had her back turned, I takes the vanilla flavoring and go outside.

Then I pour that vanilla all over me!

Well, the gnats stuck to me,

and the flies were after me,

and the bees caught sight of the flies after me

and they figured it was something good going on,

and they come in too!

Well, finally, when Grandma caught me, I mean I was doing *90 miles an hour* around the house.

"Girl! *You going to get sunstroke!*" she said.

Well, then she caught me and took a whiff of me. . . .

She said, "My God, *what have you been into?*"

And I tried to explain to her what happened.

And she said, "Well now, you dumb old thing, Aunt Sally just uses a little bit behind the ears. She don't draw gnats and flies and bees like this."

Noooo, she didn't.

She drew *men.*

Aunt Sally had five husbands. She was married *five* times. I didn't know but one husband, and that was the one she had when I was a little girl.

John Wilson was his name.

Grandpa said that John Wilson had to be the ignorantest man God ever blew breath into.

And Grandma hated him.

But she didn't let on, you know.

At first I didn't know that this man had a name, but I would hear people whisper, you know. When you're little you can get around, hear lots of things. I would hear them say, "Here comes Miss Sally and that fifth husband of hers."

Or "Here comes Miss Sally's fifth husband."

So I heard the word "fifth" all the time.

So I called him Uncle Fifth.

He didn't know why. I mean, he didn't think. I used to get on his lap and say, "*Hey, Uncle Fifth.*"

And he'd say to Pa, "Jim, I just don't know why this gal calls me Uncle Fifth."

And Pa would look over at Grandma and say, "See what I mean?"

I *loved* Aunt Sally and Uncle Fifth.

Uncle Fifth was kind of stupid, you know, but I liked him anyway. We'd go to church and Aunt Sally would walk in, with me behind her trying to walk just like her, and she'd pull into the pew. Uncle Fifth would sit on the end, she'd sit beside him, and I'd sit beside her and Grandma. Pa always sat up front.

Somebody would come over and say,

"*Hello*, Miss Sally.

"My, that's a *fine* brooch you've got on."

And Aunt Sally would know what they were looking at. She always wore long sleeves 'cause she had big arms. She'd take that fan out of her sleeve, open it up, and say, "Well, *thank you*, Mr. Jones.

"*For recognizing my brooch.*"

And my grandmother would say, "Do Jesus!"

Then she'd tell Pa at home, "That sister of yours is an out-and-out *huzzzy.*" Now, what could a four-year-old know about being a huzzzy? If they meant Aunt Sally, then *I* wanted to be a huzzzy.

I'd practice, "Huzzzy! Huzzzy! Huzzzy!"

I could see myself looking like Aunt Sally and doing what huzzzies do, whatever that was. One day a lady asked me what I wanted to be when I grew up.

"I want to be a huzzzy like my Aunt Sally."

You don't *hear* people faint, but you could hear my grandmother, "*Aahhh!*" Bam! She hit the floor.

My aunt Sally about died laughing.

Well, Grandma washed my mouth out with soap.

Didn't stop me, though.

. . . And *that's* the end of that. ✳

BECOMING A FOLKLORIST

Older children (ages 7-10) may want more of an intellectual challenge while examining their family's stories. The activities in this section let them don the hat of a professional folklorist by documenting their family's rich history through audiotape, videotape, or both. Don't necessarily think of this activity as a one-time event. Your children may decide to make this an ongoing project, continuing to document and collect the stories, anecdotes, and mannerisms of family members. Encourage them to do so. It can lead to enhanced relations with kin and an increased fascination and awareness of history. It will also do wonders for their self-esteem.

The material your children collect can be stored in a variety of ways. It can be organized into a book. It can be kept as a permanent record on audio- or videotape or it can be turned into a play, poem, or drawing. Whatever you decide to do with the gathered information, don't worry too much about turning it into a formal product or presentation. It's the process of *hearing* stories and *relating* to relatives through their personal narratives that's important here.

Remember, old traditions aren't the only ones worth collecting. As families grow, so do their customs and habits, and it's important to recognize their value, regardless of their age. Even contemporary stories, like grandpa's latest excursion to Kmart or Aunt Louise's disastrous attempt at cherry pie, are part of your newfound archive.

Be aware that the way a story is told is as important as the information in that story. Encourage your children to make a note of facial expressions, funny mannerisms, and inflections in voice tones of the people they are interviewing. Children can be extremely perceptive about minute details, and suggesting that they become avid observers not only will be fun, but also will enhance their feelings of responsibility.

The Equipment

MATERIALS: *Tape recorder, video camera, portable computer or paper and pencil*
OPTIONAL: *Camera, old photos, objects*

Audiotaping, videotaping, or note taking are the most popular and practical ways of recording family folklore. Whatever way you choose to record your subject, face-to-face contact is essential. If you're taking notes by hand or with a portable computer, try to make eye contact with your subject as much as possible. If you are filming your subject, make sure you're not behind the camera while conducting the interview. Instead, either set up the camera on a tripod ahead of time, focusing it on your subject, or bring along a family member or friend to man the camera. If you choose to use an audiotape recorder, a small cassette player with an omni-directional microphone will give good results (although if your children already have a tape player they are familiar with, they should use it). A sixty-minute cassette—thirty minutes per side—is a good choice and economical. A camera isn't necessary, though it can provide a record of the interview and will give your kids an added but enjoyable responsibility.

How to Record

The following technical guidelines, from *A Celebration of American Family Folklore* by Steve Zeitlin, Amy Kotkin, and Holly Cutting Baker, will prepare your kids for the recording process:

- Run a test ahead of time to make sure all voices, including theirs, can be picked up.
- Eliminate any extraneous noises by turning off music, closing the window, and moving away from rooms filled with chatting people.

- Have them place the camera or tape recorder where it will not be disturbed during the interview and where they will have easy access to it if it becomes necessary to change tapes.

WHO SHOULD YOUR CHILDREN INTERVIEW FIRST?

The first outside person your children should interview should be someone with whom they feel very comfortable. Interviewing is not easy, but young children usually have the greatest success with grandparents.

The most productive interviews are those that take place in a natural context—like family dinners, picnics, reunions, and holidays—when stories flow freely. Under these circumstances you might just be able to turn on your tape recorder and sit back. At the very least, your children can make a mental note of their observations and write them down later on.

ASK YOUR CHILDREN TO . . .

1. Start with a question or topic they know will elicit a full reply from their subject. An example of this might be a favorite story told by the relative they are interviewing. This will give the interviewee confidence in his ability to contribute something of value to the interview.

2. Avoid yes or no questions. Instead, have them ask evocative questions that may lead to a story. A great place to start is with memories of play. Have them conduct an activity called Memory Maps, presented earlier in this chapter, asking the relative to draw a map of the place he or she played as child and to elaborate on the memories connected with that spot.

3. Do not push too hard for answers. Sometimes, because of painful memories, forgetfulness, or embarrassment, relatives choose not to reveal certain things about their past. It's important for children to realize this and to use their discretion. Make peace with the fact that some information may never surface.

4. **Show interest.** Make sure your kids take an active part in the conversation without dominating. Learning to be a creative listener as well as questioner is the key.

5. **Let the interviewee go off on a tangent if he or she wants.** The interviewee might touch on subjects your children never thought about before.

6. **Never turn off the tape recorder or video camera unless asked.** Not only does it break concentration but also it makes the subject feel like what he or she is saying isn't important.

7. **Use objects whenever possible.** Documents, letters, photographs, albums, scrapbooks, home movies, and other family heirlooms can be wonderful tools for stimulating memories.

8. **Be sensitive to the needs of family members.** Ask your children to schedule their sessions at a convenient time. Older people tire easily, and they should stop the interview at the first sign of fatigue.

9. **Expect some relatives to be shy.** Know that while some family members will be eager to help your children on their quest, others may be more guarded. Protect their privacy. Make sure your kids explain their interest for doing the interview.

10. **If you say you will erase a tape or part of it, do so, even if it means losing important information.** Also, never record secretly. Bad feelings within the family can occur if a relative feels he or she has been taped dishonestly.

What Kinds of Questions Should My Children Ask?

The following are suggested questions, although your children should also try to come up with some of their own.

> What did your home look like as a child? Did you like living there? Did you have a happy childhood? Did you ever have a

frightening moment? How about an embarrassing one?

Do you have any nicknames? Are there any nicknames in your family? Is there a naming tradition in your family? Do you have your father's or mother's name, for example?

What do you know about your last name? Is it Italian? Spanish? African? Was it changed after your relatives came to the United States? If so, are there stories about the change?

Are there certain things in your family history you would like to know but no one will tell you?

Do you have an eccentric character in your family's past?

Did you have a best friend as a child?

Did you have a role model as a child? What about now?

What was your favorite hobby as a child? How about now?

How did your parents, grandparents, and other relatives meet and come to marry?

Did your mother or father have a first love who broke their heart? Did they break someone else's?

Are there any historical events that affected your family? For example, how did your family survive the the Civil War? Great Depression? Vietnam War? World War II? Did your parents come to America from another country? If so, why?

What expressions are used in your family? Did they come from specific incidents? Does a particular relative make up funny expressions?

How are holidays celebrated in your family? What holidays are most important?

Does your family have its own original holiday?

Does your family have any objects that have been passed down through generations? What are they?

What are the guiding principles in your life?

In dealing with others, what are some important things you've learned?

When you are feeling down, what do you like to think about?

What are the things that give you the most joy?

What is one thing your parents taught you that you can pass down to me?

What is your greatest wish?

ADOPTION

Children who are adopted often regard their adoptive parents as their only parents, and they should be encouraged to explore their adoptive family's roots through their stories. Some adoption situations can be delicate, however, such as a foster child who is sensitive to the subject. One approach is to have your adopted children try working with a fictional family instead, perhaps from a book or a film or a cartoon, when trying some of the activities listed in this chapter. Or focus on the future, instead of the past, such as in the following activity.

Time Capsule. Help your adopted children establish their own family traditions by asking them to travel into the future. Pretend it's the year 2050. Have them describe how things have changed since they were young and living in your house. Where do they live now? What kind of a family do they have? What is their neighborhood like? Which traditions have they clung to and which have they discarded? Have other family members do the same.

You should also share stories by and about other adopted children with your own. Hearing the stories of others can be incredibly reassuring, reminding your children that others have shared their experiences and have thrived.

BIBLIOGRAPHY OF ADOPTION LITERATURE

Here are a few of my favorite stories and a Web site that address adoption issues:

Ages 4–6 Years

Curtis, Jamie Lee, *Tell Me Again about the Night I Was Born* (New York: Harper-Collins, 1996).

D'Antonio, Nancy, *Our Baby from China* (Morton Grove, Ill.: Albert Whitman, 1997).

Girard, Linda Walvoord, *We Adopted You, Benjamin Koo* (Niles, Ill.: Albert Whitman, 1989).

McCully, Emily Arnold, *My Real Family* (New York: Harcourt Brace, 1994).

Myers, Walter Dean, *Me, Mop, and the Moondance* (New York: Delacorte Press, 1988).

Ages 7–8 Years

Wasson, Valentina, *The Chosen Baby* (Philadelphia: J. B. Lippincott, 1977).

Ages 8–10 Years

Krementz, Jill, *How It Feels to Be Adopted* (New York: Alfred Knopf, 1991).

Perl, Lila, *Annabelle Starr, E.S.P.* (New York: Clarion, 1983).

Warren, Andrea, *Orphan Train Riders* (New York: Houghton Mifflin, 1996).

Ages 10 Years and Older

Ashabranner, Brent, "The Lion's Whisker" in *The Lion's Whisker, and Other Ethiopian Tales* (New York: Linnet, 1997).

Web Site Recommendation

www.angelfire.com/in/AdoptionStoryteller
The Adoption Storyteller Web site presents stories of life, love, loss, and healing from an adoption perspective.

3

Gulps, Guffaws, and Giggles

How to Read Stories to Children

Books are man's rational protest against the irrational, . . . man's ideal against the world's real, . . . man's revelation of the God within him.
JOHN COWPER POWYS, *The Enjoyment of Literature*

Each summer, when the crickets gather outside my window for their annual reunion and I hear the distant chimes of the roving ice cream truck, I'm transported to the neighborhood of my youth. My cousin lived down the block from me, and we spent our childhood climbing up and down the hill that separated our homes. Our afternoons were spent in my backyard, jumping around for hours in the cool sprinkler. Nights were reserved for slumber parties at her house.

Thirty years have passed since the two of us stayed awake all night giggling and gossiping, but there are certain memories that won't fade: the crisp floral sheets on the guest bed I always slept in; the white cereal bowls filled with cornflakes and wheat germ that awaited us in the morning; and the utter delight we felt each time my Aunt Blanka read to us before turning out the light.

My aunt only read us Dr. Seuss books. In fact, I can't even recall seeing any other books in my cousin's room. Yet somehow, we didn't mind hearing *The Cat in the Hat* or *Green Eggs and Ham* over and over again. We got to know the rhymes by heart and would recite them along with my aunt. The repetition was comforting to me, like an old friend whose behavior was predictable but never boring. But those read-aloud evenings did more than simply entertain. They jump-started our imaginations, endowed us with playful language, and left us with a love of story. They showed us that the world extended beyond our backyards and taught us about life's infinite possibilities.

From *The Cat in the Hat* we learned to suspend cynicism by embracing dancing goldfish, runaway kites, and blue-haired men named Thing One and Thing Two. It was okay to express ourselves playfully by sporting an enormous floppy hat, using nonsensical words, and letting a magical machine steamroll through our living room. But we also learned that with every choice comes a consequence. Running amok with a spontaneous feline is fun. Cleaning up its mess is more complicated.

It would be great if we orally passed all our stories to our children. But for those of us who haven't yet figured out how to access or share them, *reading* our favorite stories can be the next best thing. We know for a fact that reading aloud to children builds their vocabulary, improves reading and writing skills, stimulates creativity, and bonds adult and child. The Commission on Reading, funded by the U.S. Department of Education, stressed that the foremost single activity for building knowledge for eventual success is reading aloud. Scientists have even linked increased brain activity in children in the womb to being read to during pregnancy. But there are other, more profound benefits to reading aloud rarely measured by researchers. Hearing stories shapes our lives, helping us make sense of our past and present experience, while allowing us to imagine possibilities for ourselves for the future. Daniel Taylor, an English professor and the author of *The Healing Power of Stories*, suggests that our ability to see ourselves as something more and better than we presently are is dependent on our story-making abilities. It derives from the power of the imagination to see and believe future stories for ourselves in which our lives are rich and meaningful.

This chapter is not about strengthening your children's reading skills. It's about strengthening their story skills. By building a story-rich home, you'll be constructing an invaluable framework within which your kids can live. You'll be giving them plot lines to emulate, heroes to model themselves after, villains to test their values. And you'll be helping them to see their own lives in perspective. Jim Trelease, the author of *The Read-Aloud Handbook*, has suggested that by filling your kids' heads with stories about other people's experiences, you increasingly enable them to say, "Hey, the same thing happened to me. I'm not alone."

A child is never too young to be read to. Just as you talk to your newborn daughter without expecting her to understand you, so should you feel free to read to her. Children of any age will benefit from the sound of your voice, the expressiveness of your face, your one-on-one presence.

PREPARING TO READ ALOUD

Before you begin to read, there are a few things to remember.

1. Resist the temptation to teach. Remember that this is about sharing a story with your children, not achieving a better reading score. Let the learning happen naturally, by letting them do their own problem solving. It's very important not to interrupt a story midway to ask an instructive question like, "That story takes place in Miami. Do you remember where Miami is on the map?" We've become so consumed with factual truths that we forget that in the world of stories, emotional truths play as important a role. If you interrupt the story to convey outside facts, you disrupt your children's emotional connection to the characters and action. This doesn't mean you shouldn't respond to the questions your children may ask while you read. But give them room to analyze a story in their own unique way and to draw their own conclusions and observations.

> If you deny your children the freedom to find meaning for them-
> selves in your stories, you are defeating yourself as well. The price
> you pay is a bored, indifferent child or, even worse, a child who
> deeply resents the limits you constantly put on his or her freedom.
> And what happens then, I think, is that the child preserves this
> resentment, like a pickle in a jar of vinegar, in the form of self-pity.
> CHASE COLLINS, *Tell Me a Story*

2. Don't worry too much about the content of a story. My philosophy is, if you don't like it, change it. If the writing in a particular book isn't rich enough for me, I embellish it with adjectives. If a story has an unsavory character, I make him more likable, perhaps through the voice I give him, or in the way I change his plot line. Storybooks are mere skeletons. The embellishments and twists you bring to the reading create the full body of a story.

You may like a particular author's use of language and rhythm and feel that changing it around destroys the integrity of the writing. If that's the case, don't do it. Nobody wants you to alter something you hold dear. But one approach you might consider is to read the book exactly as it is written several times, until your kids are familiar with the original version. Then tell them it's time for some fun by saying, "I love this book, but I think there could be different endings to the story. Let's rewrite the ending using the author's language and rhythms."

> A lot of books have a good premise but a bad execution. I find that by keeping the premise but changing the storyline, I can have fun. There are no sacred cows in storytelling.
>
> JACOB B.

3. Make this a participatory experience. Before you even begin reading, you can get your kids involved by asking them to put on their imaginary storytelling hats and reacting to their creations. "Hey, your hat has an enormous feather sticking out of it and it's tickling my nose!" you might say. Or, "Look! You've just put a crown on your head. Are you the king of the neighborhood?" Look for any opportunity to elicit sounds, voices, and ideas from the people to whom you are reading.

4. Don't read too quickly. One of the reasons I love watching the British perform Shakespeare is because they take their time delivering each word. They linger, indulging in the richness of the language. Reading slowly doesn't diminish your children's enjoyment. On the contrary, the more time you take, the better they'll be able to visualize the story. Would you rush past the Mona Lisa at the Louvre, or would you take the time to study it? Treat the language in your book like a visual portrait. Each word creates a new stroke of the paintbrush and a new picture for your kids to absorb. It's better to only get through one-third of a book, taking time to answer your children's questions and delight in the story's language and characters, than to rush through the entire book in order to finish.

5. Don't turn the pages too quickly. Slow down!!! It takes lots of time for your children to digest everything on the page. You may have completed a passage about a red rooster crossing the road, but your children will still be looking at the dotted yellow line in the middle of the road, the funny looking feather that fell off the rooster's back, the Jeep that is driving on the *other* side of the road, the child that is staring at all of this in the far right corner of the illustration, and the apple tree that hovers over the child who is staring. One way to assure you're not moving along too quickly is by asking your children to be page turners. That way, they will have an active part in the storytelling process and will turn the page after they have digested everything they need to see.

6. Don't use a book as a threat. Follow the suggestion of reading-aloud advocate Jim Trelease and avoiding saying things like, "If you don't clean up your room, no story tonight!" As soon as your children see that you've turned the book into a weapon, they'll change their attitude about books from positive to negative.

7. Try not to read stories that you don't like. Your distaste for them will come out, even if you try to hide it.

8. Make sure everyone has an equal view of the illustrations. "He can see the pictures better than I can!" is a familiar refrain for anyone who has read aloud to young kids. You can avoid this argument at the onset by positioning yourself equally between your kids, if possible.

9. If your kids are more than three years apart in age, read to them individually. Although life would undoubtedly be simpler by reading the same book to all your kids at once, if there's a substantial age difference between them, you'll only be courting trouble by combining your read-aloud sessions. Either the oldest will get bored or the youngest will become distressed. Challenging your children is good; frustrating them is not. Take the extra time necessary and read an age-appropriate book to each child.

10. Don't stop reading aloud to your kids once they learn to read. Reading aloud should continue as long as possible, even after a child has learned to read. Not only will it help your kids excel in their math and verbal skills, but also it will create and seal a special bond with your children.

I'm convinced that my passion for books was fueled by the stories my dad read to me as a kid. He would read histories to me about the ancient Romans, the Israelites, the Greeks, and I loved them. Now as a book editor, I feel I've returned to my first love. I've returned home.

JULIA S.

MAKING WRITTEN STORIES EVEN MORE FUN

Embellishing Text

Don't be afraid to embellish texts, whether they be nursery rhymes or entire storybooks. If you're reading "Jack and Jill," maybe *red-headed* Jack and *freckle-faced* Jill *skipped* up the hill to fetch a *bright yellow* pail of water. Perhaps they *galloped* up the hill on a giggling horse, or maybe Jack *pulled* Jill in his new red wagon.

If you feel the pace of the story is slowed down too much by your new adjectives, try embellishing verbs, which will keep the action moving; for example, Jack and Jill *ran furiously* up the hill, to fetch a pail of water, Jack fell and *rolled and rolled and rolled down the steep hill,* and Jill came tumbling after.

ENHANCE GENERAL DESCRIPTIONS

Many words don't translate that well to small kids because they haven't had the life experience from which to create images. If a story describes one of the characters as "happy," take it farther. Make her so happy that she danced and sang aloud in the middle of a mall. If a character is tall, make him so tall, that when he stood on his toes, he banged his head on the tree in the backyard. Don't rely solely on illustrations to create a visual picture for your kids. Use descriptive words and extra sentences to create a multicolored, multidimensional story.

For example, in *Lyle, Lyle, Crocodile* by Bernard Waber, the actual text is as follows:

This is the house. The house on East 88th Street. Mr. and Mrs. Primm and their son Joshua live in the house on East 88th Street. So does Lyle. Listen: SWISH, SWASH, SPLASH, SWOOSH! That's Lyle . . . Lyle, the crocodile.

Embellished, the text might read as follows:

This is the house. The *tall brownstone* on East 88th Street in *noisy, bustling New York City.* Mr. and Mrs. Primm, *who were as skinny as licorice,* and their son, *a curly-haired giggler* named Joshua, live in the house on East 88th Street. So does Lyle. Listen: SWISH, SWASH, SPLASH, SWOOSH! That's Lyle . . . Lyle, the crocodile.

PERSONALIZE EACH STORY

One of the best ways to hook your kids on a story is to relate it to their own lives. Try embellishing with descriptions that mirror your kids' lives. For example,

This is the house. The house on East 88th Street. Mr. and Mrs. Primm, *who loved to fill their home with (name an object that sits in your own home),* and their son, Joshua, *who collected (list a few objects also collected by your child),* live in the house on East 88th Street. So does Lyle. Listen: SWISH, SWASH, SPLASH, SWOOSH! That's Lyle . . . Lyle, the crocodile.

Again, if you're concerned about destroying the integrity of a book by changing its language, read the original text to your children first and then let them know you are embellishing it for fun. Children love making a story their very own.

EMBELLISHING RHYMING STORIES

If you love the rhyming aspect of a story and don't want to change it, you can embellish in rhyme. Look for an opportunity within the story where you can deviate without interfering with the plot line. One trick that I always use when I'm looking for ways to embellish texts is to create lists. I always look for any opportunity in a text that lends itself to such rosters. Let me show you an example of how to use lists to embellish a rhyming story for *The Cat in the Hat*. The actual text is as follows:

> "I know some good games we could play,"
> Said the cat.
> "I know some new tricks,"
> Said the Cat in the Hat.
> "A lot of good tricks.
> I will show them to you.
> Your mother
> Will not mind at all if I do."

Now let's embellish the text by inserting a list of games and tricks the Cat in the Hat could play:

> *We could play cards or we could play tag.*
> *We could make puppets with only a bag.*
> *We could go skating or boating or not.*
> *We could go out once the weather gets hot.*

Better yet, ask your kids to come up with their own rhymes. For example, when Thing One and Thing Two begin flying a kite around the house and knocking over everything in sight, ask your kids, "What else went flying around the room?" You can start them off with the beginning of a sentence and ask them to complete it in rhyme:

We saw dad's hat.
*And we saw a*_____.
We saw mom's car.
*And we saw a*_____.

Suggestions for Embellishing Stories

1. Ask for sound effects. Kids love to participate and are willing to make sounds for just about anything, whether it be people, animals, or inanimate objects. Eliciting sounds from your kids will hold their attention while making them feel like they are active participants in the storytelling process.

Don't just ask for the obvious sounds, like the "bah" of a sheep or the "whsssh" of the wind. Look for sounds in places you normally wouldn't. How would a purple crayon sound as it swirls in circles in *Harold and the Purple Crayon*? What noises would a pumpkin carriage make as it motors home from the ball in *Cinderella*? What would the one-hundred-year-old snore of *Rip Van Winkle* sound like?

2. Put your body into the story. Engaging physically in a story is a wonderful way to elicit participation from your kids, as long as you set limits. If you're outside, you might want to let your kids get up and be active. But reading times often take place during quieter periods like bedtime, and the last thing you'll want to do is to get your kids riled up when it's time for them to go to sleep.

So how do you get your kids to be physical while still keeping them in one place? Here are a few tricks that work like a charm: If a character in one of my stories is running, I merely move my arms back and forth while panting. If one of the characters in my story is jumping, I lower my head and raise it up with a jumping-on-the-bed kind of sound like "weeeeeee!" If someone is driving a car, I take the steering wheel and pretend to sharply turn the wheel, thrusting my body sharply to one side. Containing your kids physically during a read-aloud session won't squelch their spirits. On the contrary, the less space your kids have to move in, the more their imaginations will compensate and the better they'll be able to focus on the story. Here's an excerpt from *The Snowy Day* by Ezra Jack Keats:

One winter morning Peter woke up and looked out the window. Snow had fallen during the night. It covered everything as far as he could see. After breakfast he put on his snowsuit and ran outside.

I've added in body movements and some other details to show you how to bring a physical dimension to your story:

One winter morning Peter woke up . . .

Say to your kids, "*Pretend you're sleeping and when you hear the alarm clock, wake up. Ready? Rrrrrrrrrrrring!!!!*"

. . . and looked out the window.

Pretend to pull aside the curtains and peer outside.

Snow had fallen during the night. It covered everything as far as he could see. After breakfast . . .

Add, "*which included a bowl of cereal (pretend to slurp cereal), bananas (peel imaginary banana and fling it over your shoulder, if you want to be silly), and a glass of milk ("glup glup glup" you say as you drink),*"

. . . he put on his snowsuit and ran outside.

You can continue to elaborate by asking your children to hand you a snowsuit. Wait for them to throw an imaginary snowsuit, then have fun by saying, "That's a diaper, not a snow suit. I need a snow suit." Wait for them to throw you another imaginary object. "That's a hamburger, not a snow suit," and so on. You and your kids can pretend to be Peter, trying on the snowsuit for size. Perhaps it's too tight and you are forced to huff and puff while putting it on. Or you can pretend that it originally belonged to an elephant, and you get lost finding your way in the acres of fabric.

3. Modulate your voice. Just the slightest changes in your voice can cause an outbreak of giggles during bedtime readings. Try changing it according to the characters and incidents in the book. Why not stretch your voice by elongating your words each time Pinocchio's nose grows, or drop your head, yawn, and read sluggishly when Winnie the Pooh starts to fall asleep? Remember, there are more ways to change your voice than simply raising or lowering it. Try reading a passage from a book as if you were from another country or mimic a famous television personality.

> My father is an immigrant from Italy, but his accent isn't really detectable since he came to America as a small boy. But when he would read to me as a child, the cadence of the Italian language would come out a little and I loved it. It was the only time I really got a sense of where he was from.
>
> LISA T.

4. Pay attention to speed and tempo. Another trick every professional storyteller uses is tempo variation. During a one-woman show I performed, I ran across the problem of holding the audience's attention. The material was quite serious, and patches in the monologue were fairly lengthy. How could I hold onto my audience and keep them from getting distracted, I wondered. I looked for an area in my monologue that reflected a change in my emotional state, and during that passage, sped up the delivery considerably. The sudden speed, accompanied by a raised voice, lured my audience back to me.

Speeding up or slowing down during a reading can be an extremely powerful tool for ensnaring your listeners. But it's only effective if you use the tempo changes sparingly. Pick out areas where it makes sense to do it, such as during a character's emotional highs or lows; during any kind of movement, like a car, train, or plane ride; or during a character's slow time, like when he's sleeping or loafing. Changing the tempo not only will excite your listeners, but also will keep you from getting bored, especially if this is the hundredth time of reading the same story.

5. Use silences. The hardest thing for me to master as a storyteller has been the use of silence. When you're standing alone on a stage, your instinct is to say something! But experience has taught me that when telling a story, silence can be more powerful than words.

To the storyteller, silence isn't simply the absence of words. It can imply sadness, pain, fright, comfort, or victory. It can be used to magnify the sentence that's about to come next or to punctuate the preceding one. Or it can become a beat that concludes a rhythm.

Professional storytellers use silence to manipulate their audiences and so should you. Choose an area in the text to which you want to draw attention, and instead of reading it as usual, pause and become totally silent for a second, before carrying on with the story. If you really want to create suspense, make direct eye contact with your children during that silence. You'll be amazed how drawn in your kids will be.

6. Act it out. There's nothing kids love better than to perform stories. Start to read, and each time a new character is introduced, ask your child to become that character, doing exactly what the story calls for. If your son is the Grinch From *The Grinch That Stole*

Christmas, have him pretend to hoard his possessions, laugh fiendishly, scour for money, or mope. Don't worry if you run out of characters. Just have your kids act out inanimate objects, like the sun or the moon, a tree or even a chair! Whatever the object, person, or animal, your children will be delighted to act it out.

7. Rock 'n' roll it! Instead of reading, try singing a familiar story to your kids one night. Or ask your kids to do it. How would Madonna recite Maurice Sendak's *Where the Wild Things Are*? Or Michael Jackson? How about the opera singer Plácido Domingo? Be silly and they're sure to follow.

8. Substitute silly words. If you've read a certain book many times and your child is familiar with the text, try substituting a silly word in place of the real one. For example, you might read, "Jack and Jill/Went up the hill/To fetch a pail of *lemonade.*" Inevitably, your child will correct you and laugh while doing it. It's a great way to keep her attention while developing her listening skills.

Can I apply this activity to other types of stories? Substituting words can be used with stories that are too violent or scary or whose language is outdated. Simply substitute your word for the word in the story. Better yet, if you run across a word or sentence you feel uncomfortable with, have your kids substitute a better one.

9. Invite a guest. If guests are visiting, see if they might be willing to read a story to your kids. Children love to hear stories told with different voices and intonations, and grandparents, older siblings, or family friends can offer variety and spice to a read-aloud session.

10. Use audio cassettes or CDs. Although recorded stories can never compete with a live reading, they can introduce your children to a wide range of storytelling styles and traditions. You can use them during car trips, after or during dinner, before school, or at bedtime. Hearing other storytellers on tape will be a great treat for your kids and a welcome reprieve for you.

My little boy, Jesse, was 16 months old the first time he listened to *Peter and the Wolf.* The music enchanted him. He did not interrupt with a sound of his own, and he did not move, except to slip onto my lap for protection from the wolf who comes from the forest to eat the duck and chomp the bird and do God-knows-what to the little boy, Peter.

I only had to walk by the stereo cabinet and he ran to me and hung from my leg: "Pe'r Woof! Pe'r Woof!" Okay, okay. I would hit the green button. The speakers popped. The anticipation sent him into the air, then into my arms. Our position was always the same: I sat on the sofa, and he straddled my lap, jammed his arms between my stomach and his, and pressed his cheek against my chest. And he wouldn't move, wouldn't make a sound from beginning to end, except for a whisper at the ominous turn in the score, at the height of his fear: "Woof coming!"

One afternoon, I couldn't sit and listen with him. He cast his eyes at the toys on the floor of the kitchen. "Okay," he said. "Me listen with my sheep." He picked up the sheep and put it under one arm. "My dog, my alligator!" Yes, the ferocious alligator! He sat himself at the end of the sofa, fast against the fat upholstered arm, with the sheep on one side of him, the dog next to the sheep, and the alligator on his lap. And from then on, whenever he wanted to hear *Peter and the Wolf,* he gathered these three friends and arranged himself and them just so.

Once, I saw him whisper to the sheep. He saw me seeing him. "Me p'ect them," he explained. Me protect them. He had taken my role. What a victory in his little life!

FRAN SNYDER, mother of Anna, 8, and Jesse, 6

You can acquire storytelling tapes through your local library or school or at most major bookstores (in the audiobook section). In addition, the National Association for the Preservation and Perpetuation of Storytelling (NAPPS) can send you a copy of The National Storytelling Catalogue and a list of other resources available to you. For information, write to NAPPS, P.O. Box 309, Jonesborough, Tennessee 37659.

Or consider making your own tape. Simply read aloud from your child's favorite books. These tapes can keep your child company in your absence.

> Last Easter, I was in Argentina for 10 days. So for every night I'd be gone, I left [my kids] a tape of an Easter story I'd read. I went through the Last Supper and then what Easter Sunday was all about. I would ask, "Now, are you in your bed?" And apparently they would say, "Yes, Mummy." What was really good for me to hear was when, for the first time, Beatrice said, "Oh, sorry, Mummy, I didn't listen to the story Thursday night." Which meant she didn't need to. She felt secure. I was really pleased for that.
>
> SARAH FERGUSON, DUCHESS OF YORK,
> in *Working Woman* magazine

11. Choose your own ending. Read the first few lines of a familiar book, then close it and make up the rest of the story with your children.

What Happens If My Child Can't Think of Anything to Add to the Story?

Acceptance is the key ingredient in all the exercises. If you ask your children to make up the ending of a story and they can't think of anything, assume it's because they are guarders of a secret. If you ask them what kind of imaginary story hat they are wearing and all they can say is "I don't know," assume it's an I DON'T KNOW hat and any time someone asks a question while they're wearing that hat, they have to answer, "I don't know." You can also help them by asking for ideas incrementally. For example, instead of asking them to come up with an ending for an entire story, just have them supply one word. By using their responses, however primitive or complex, you are subtly showing your stamp of approval. Giving your children the license to come up with their own ideas does wonders for their self-esteem, as well as their imaginations.

What Happens If My Child Keeps Asking for the Same Story Over and Over Again?

There's no rhyme or reason as to why children choose a certain story over another one. It may be identification with a character or a plot line to which they can relate. It may be a way for them to process new information or relive events in their mind and sort them out. Or, they may simply enjoy a rhythm's repetition, which can be comforting, like a meditative chant. No doubt about it, your children will request certain stories again and again.

How Can I Remain Interested in a Story I Have Told Twenty Times Before?

There are two things I generally recommend to parents. The first is to choose stories that you adore, so reading them for the four-hundredth time doesn't feel like you're suffering a slow fingernail torture. You should also have a large enough store of books from which to choose so when your child says, "How about reading me *The Cat in the Hat* again?" you can say, "What about *Green Eggs and Ham?*" But suppose your child insists on *The Cat in the Hat?* What happens if, no matter what you suggest, your child is fixated on the one story you've read into the ground. What should you do? *Pretend* as hard as you can to love it, that it's the most interesting book you've ever read. Believe it or not, before long, you will be interested.

It's important to remember, however, that children sometimes use books like security blankets. Jim Trelease points out in *The Read-Aloud Handbook* that "a child may remember that last night his mother read *Goodnight, Moon* before abandoning him to the dark and somehow made it to morning and nothing scary came in through the window to drag him out of bed and into the woods, so the next night and the next he requests it as a sort of insurance policy." Also, children may ask you to read a passage again and again as a way of clarifying a particular segment, rather than asking you to stop and explain it to them.

MAKING THE MOST OUT OF ILLUSTRATIONS

There's more to a picture than meets the eye. Behind every illustration are a thousand stories, and it's up to you and your children to find them. Treat every object in a picture as a place where stories hide.

In this picture from *The Little Engine That Could,* we see a giraffe, a clown, a duck, some dancing dolls, and a steam engine. We also see a trees and bushes in the distance, and a few twinkling stars in the sky. Each one of these objects has a story to tell and their perspective might shed new light on the story.

Step into the Picture! Climb into the picture and ask your daughter to become an object in the picture, like the dress of one of the dancing dolls. Ask her to describe what life is like as a dress. Have your son become the ear of the giraffe or the beak of the duck and have him describe his daily habits and observations.

Retell It! Retell *The Little Engine That Could* from the different perspectives of each of the characters in the picture. How would the clown read the story? How would he tell it in his own words?

Change the Story. Create an entirely new story based on the illustration, by passing it from one person to the next. As the story comes to you, add to the original story.

Illustration Game. Tell the story behind the following illustrations.

The Artist in You. Resist showing your child the illustrations in a new book. Instead, have her draw her own, either during or after your reading. Or ask your child to draw pictures based on the following paragraphs from popular books:

Make Way for Ducklings by Robert McCloskey

One day the ducklings hatched out. First came Jack, then Kack, and then Lack, then Mack and Nack and Ouack and Pack and Quack. Mr. and Mrs. Mallard were bursting with pride. It was a great responsibility taking care of so many ducklings, and it kept them very busy.

Through the Looking Glass, and What Alice Found There
by Lewis Carroll

Beware the Jabberwock, my son!
The jaws that bite, the claws that catch!
Beware the Jubjub bird, and shun
The frumious Bandersnatch!

A Chair for My Mother by Vera B. Williams

My mother and I were coming home from buying new shoes. I had new sandals. She had new pumps. We were walking to our house from the bus. We were looking at everyone's tulips. She was saying she liked red tulips and I was saying I liked yellow ones. Then we came to our block.

Become the Picture. Start to read your child a story but don't show him any of the accompanying illustrations. Instead, have your child act out the pictures at random points during the reading. Here's how the game works: Let your child know he'll be illustrating the read-aloud session with his body and clear away a physical space for him, even if it's a small area on his bed. Begin reading. Like in the game of musical chairs, whenever you stop reading, he must illustrate that section of the book through body movements and facial expressions. Don't limit the game to places in the book where pictures already exist. Stop your reading whenever you feel like it and have fun watching your child paint new possibilities.

PUTTING IT ALL TOGETHER

Now let's look at ways to combine the elements I've discussed thus far by retelling a few paragraphs from *A Boy Named Ray*, a story I wrote back in 1987 about reuse and recycling. It's a story that always works well with young children, particularly since the rhymes calm them down and refocus them.

When I tell it, I try to elicit audience participation at every turn and I've outlined exactly how I do it. You needn't feel compelled to jump around like I do, but hopefully, the examples in this story will give you some new ideas for evoking participation.

A Boy Named Ray

❈ (I begin by making my audience put on their storytelling hats which, I tell them, grow in their ears. "Look at yours," I say to a child. "Why it's sprouting purple beans!" "And yours," I say to another. "It's filled with diamonds that are sparkling so brightly, I have to put my sunglasses on just to view it." Now that the kids know they've been given a license to be silly and imaginative, I ask them to describe their storytelling hats to me. Once they've all had a chance to tell me about their hats, I begin.) ❈

There once was a boy named Ray.
He was given a bright pink ball of clay
He would play all day with the clay

"Can you please throw me a ball of clay?" I ask. (I catch it and say "Thanks!" before continuing.)

And the way he would play
Was filled with joy

What a wonderful toy for a boy named Ray
Pink clay

He would mold it and shape it

"Help me mold it." I say, and begin miming a stretchy piece of clay.

Poke it and pick it

*I mime poking it while making a funny poking noise like "blop blop
blop blop blop."*

Bounce it and kick it

I pretend to bounce it and when I kick it I go "binggggggggggggg!"

Stick it on his nose
And on the ends of his toes

*I mime pulling the gooey clay off of my nose and toes, like chewing
gum.*

Hang it from his chin

Mime it hanging from chin.

And then grin with joy
What a wonderful toy for a boy named Ray
Pink clay.

Then one day
Ray's mother said, "Ray!"

I say it, rolling my r's :
"RRRRRRRRRRRRRRRRRRRAY!"

"You can't play with that clay."

*I wave my finger at an imaginary Ray as I say
the mom's lines, making her into a strict 1930s school-marm type.*

"It's all dirty and gray.
Just look at the way
It's all hard and it's dry.

Now you say bye-bye
And don't cry."

And she picked up the clay
And threw it away.

*I let my face quiver until I slowly begin a bigger-than-life wail and
tell all the kids to cry along with me. "Waaaaa!!! Waaaaaaa!
Waaaaah!"*

Ray began to weep.
And without making a peep
He snuck into the kitchen
And stuck his hand in the garbage pail.

*I sneak over to a child in the audience, mold her arms into a circle,
held in front of her body, then stick my hand inside that circle, as if
I'm poking around the garbage can. Then I say, "Ooh, gooey eggshells.
A clump of dried spaghetti. What else did he find in the garbage can?
Dog food? Yes, yuck. Old pieces of newspaper? You're right. Anything
else? (Accept their answers, no matter how silly or disgusting.) Yes, the
ball of clay!"*

He whisked it away
And stuck it under his hat

We mime sticking clay under our hats.

There it sat
A hard blob on his head
And he headed for bed.

FAIRY TALES

A leprechaun is of more value to the Earth than is a Prime Minister.
JAMES STEPHENS

When I was a senior at college, *feminism* was the word of choice on
campus. Night after night I sat with artsy, outspoken women on

the floor of our dorm rooms, discussing the sad state of women's affairs in America: the failure of the Equal Rights Amendment to pass in Congress, the appalling disparity between men's and women's wages, and the demeaning way women were portrayed in literature. "Take Cinderella," I said. "She couldn't get her act together until Prince Charming saved her." My friends agreed. We hated that story and the others like it that encouraged passivity by perpetuating the myth of the helpless woman.

It's been twenty years since I flexed my feminist muscle on the cold floor of my dorm room. In retrospect, I'm not sure I was right. True, glass slippers don't come in my size and never will. But I think I knew that all along. Even when my mother read to me the age-old classics, I knew I had about as much chance of landing a prince as my bicycle had of turning into a pumpkin. Maybe I was cynical before my time, but I doubt it. I enjoyed *Cinderella*, but never felt brainwashed by it. I never felt compelled to wait for a prince to save me because of the role models in my own life. My mother ran her own business, spoke her mind, and when she wanted something, went out and got it. Because of the example my mother set through her actions, I viewed Cinderella's story as a charming, albeit unrealistic one. I was able to discern between fantasy and reality, while embracing both.

I loved fairy tales growing up, although I can't say they didn't scare me. I'm still rattled by the wolf in *Little Red Riding Hood*. His fanged image, cloaked in a grandmother's shawl, etched an indelible image in my imagination. So did the mean stepmother who abandoned Hansel and Gretel and left them in the woods to die. When the big bad wolf huffed and puffed, I imagined my own house blowing down. And when Cinderella's evil stepsisters made her do all the dirty work around the house, I wondered if my own sibling might some day turn against me.

But these stories also taught me about ingenuity. When Hansel and Gretel became entrapped by a mean witch, they cleverly figured out a way to escape from her clutches. After Jack outwitted the giant, villains of any size seemed conquerable. More importantly, fairy tales stuffed my mind with fantastical imagery—of ominous forests, shaded with secrets and magic; of talking animals and enchanted trees; of human frailty and superhuman courage. To this day, the stories I tell are informed, in some measure, by those gripping pictures.

Psychologists generally recognize that fairy tales can be tremendous tools for aiding in personality development. In his landmark book, *The Uses of Enchantment*, Bruno Bettelheim suggests that "more can be learned from [fairy tales] about the inner problems of human beings, and of right solutions to their predicaments in any society, than from any other type of story within a child's comprehension." But many parents and mental health professionals alike believe that fairy tales also transmit undesirable psychological messages. The characters are often stereotyped. Villains and heroes alike use gratuitous violence. Women, for the most part, are depicted as fragile. Men usually do the saving. They typically end with ". . . and they lived happily ever after," a line that encourages us to expect perfect marriages. And we all know perfection doesn't exist.

While many of these criticisms are valid, I still think it would be a shame to eliminate fairy tales from the lives of your children. Ruth Sawyer, an early twentieth-century storyteller, says in *The Way of the Storyteller:*

> There is no reason to bar from the vigorous and buoyant minds of normal children legitimate folk experiences and fancies. Not that I champion Red Riding Hood or the Three Bears as great stories. But I do champion the cause of leaving healthy minds free, ungyved and soaring. I do hold it to be foolish and dangerous for adults to distrust this freedom for children, while they themselves distrust the substance and values of folk literature.

Dr. Richard Gardner, a child psychiatrist and the author of *Fairy Tales for Today's Children*, believes that while fairy tales are extremely powerful vehicles for transmitting messages to children, some are filled with elements that are unhealthy and maladaptive. However, rather than throwing out thousands of years of story-telling tradition, he believes we should try to use what is beneficial in these stories and downplay or discard what is not. For example, in Dr. Gardner's original adaptation of *Cinderella* (included at the end of this chapter), the heroine is not rescued by a prince or a fairy godmother, but finds her own solutions to her problems.

In the end, you know your children better than any outside expert. If you loved a particular fairy tale as a child, you'll undoubt-edly transmit that joy to your offspring. How they respond, whether fearfully or joyfully or a combination of the two, can only be gauged by you. However, there are some general guidelines of which you may want to take note.

I've found that the best time to introduce fairy tales to your kids is between the ages of 5 and 10 years. Some kids like to continue hearing them through their teens. Many will naturally make the next leap to stories that are more sophisticated, like science fiction or young-adult fiction.

As far as being too scary, again, you'll have to be the judge. But as Ann Pelowski points out in *The Family Storytelling Handbook*:

> In most cases children need and want a certain amount of scari-ness, in the years from about six and up. They want to show that they have learned to conquer their fears, or they want to identi-fy with some hero or heroine who has done so. If you leave out the terrible things from fairy tales, then you must also leave out the great good things that can conquer this terror: courage and resourcefulness in the face of evil, sacrifice that can bring well-being and happiness, faithfulness to a belief or a person, and many more. And it is just these qualities that all of us most need to see in our heroes and heroines.

I like to combine fairy tales. I start off with the Goldilocks story and weave Little Red Riding Hood and Babar into the storyline, and my son loves it.

One of my stories might sound like this: "Once upon a time Hansel, Gretel, and Berford were in the forest scattering crumbs, when they came to a house with a 'For Sale' sign on it. They were curious and went inside the house. Three bowls of porridge were on the table. Hansel tried the first bowl and said, 'This porridge is much too hot!' Gretel tried the second bowl and said, 'This porridge is much too cold!' But Berford's was just right and he ate it all up. Then they went upstairs and tried out the beds. Hansel said, 'This bed is too hard!' Gretel said, 'This one is too soft!' Berford said, 'This bed would be just right but grandma's in it! What big eyes you have grandma!' 'The better to see you with,' she answered Berford. 'What a big nose you have,' said Hansel. 'The better to smell you with,' she answered Hansel. 'What a big mouth you have!' said Gretel. 'The better to eat you with!!!!' she answered Gretel and opened her mouth wide and tried to chomp down on her. Why, it wasn't grandma at all, it was the wolf!!!! Hansel, Gretel, and Berford ran out of the house and into the woods until they had lost the wolf. They started to head home when who came bounding out of the forest but Babar, the elephant. And that leads us to our next story."

ADAM BROWN, father of Jacob, $5^{1}/_{2}$

If certain phrases are too frightening, try applying some of the techniques I discussed earlier in this chapter, like substituting your own words for the problematic ones or changing the story's ending. You can also transform a scary fairy tale into a humorous one by giving frightening characters, like witches or foxes, funny voices or adding outlandish facial expressions and gesticulations. Or ask your child to tell the fairy tale from the perspective of one of those scary characters, thereby empowering him and diminishing the characters hold on him.

If you like, let your child help you in creating an entirely new fairy tale. One of the ways to do that is by asking him detailed questions at different points throughout the story. How often does Cinderella have to polish her glass slippers? What flavor bread crumbs did Hansel and Gretel use when they scattered them throughout the forest, chocolate or cinnamon? Was Sleeping Beauty as tall and skinny as a popsicle stick or as short as a shoe? Did her Prince Charming ride a talking horse? If so, what did it talk about? And what about Snow White? Is it true she liked to nibble on cookies while tap dancing? Based on your child's answers, go back and retell the story in your own, unique way.

You may want to look for different versions of popular fairy tales. For example, a Cinderella-type story exists in many cultures, including Japanese and Egyptian, to name two. The original Cinderella wore fur slippers, which somehow turned into glass during the translation. Reading alternate versions of a fairy tale can pave the way for a fabulous discussion about values in different cultures.

Following are two versions of the Cinderella story: "Cinderelma," a contemporary tale in *Fairy Tales for Today's Children* by Dr. Richard Gardner, and my retelling of a traditional Native American tale called *The Indian Cinderella*.

Cinderelma
by DR. RICHARD GARDNER

❋ Once upon a time there was a girl named Elma. Her mother had died and on her deathbed she had given Elma a beautiful ring with a ruby red heart on it.

Elma kept the ring in a secret place. But whenever she was sad she would take it out and put it on. Just looking at the ring made her think of her dead mother who had been good to her—and she would then feel better.

Soon after Elma's mother had died, Elma's father had married again. But instead of being nice like her real mother, the stepmother was mean, and old, and ugly. She had two daughters who were also mean and ugly.

What a sad time it was for Elma! She saw very little of her father because he had so much to do. And her stepmother and stepsister sat around all day admiring their clothes and saying nasty things to her.

Elma had to wait on them hand and foot. She did the cooking, cleaning, sewing, gardening, and all the other work that had to be done. When she finished her daily work she was so tired, she would sit by the fireplace next to the ashes and cinders and fall asleep. Because of this the stepsisters began calling her Cinderelma.

Now it happened that the King ordered a great celebration which was to last for two days. He invited all the maidens in the kingdom so that his only son, the Prince, could select the bride.

Cinderelma's stepsisters were very excited. They could think of nothing more wonderful than marrying the Prince and for weeks they talked only of what they would wear to the ball. But Cinderelma was very sad. She knew she would never be allowed to go.

Finally the first day of the celebration arrived. Cinderelma worked very hard helping her stepsisters and stepmother dress and fix their hair.

After they left for the ball, Cinderelma sat in the kitchen and began to cry. She wanted so much to go she began thinking how wonderful it would be if suddenly a fairy godmother appeared and would give her everything she wanted.

She would ask the fairy godmother to change her rags into a magnificent dress made of gold thread with beautiful jewels all over it.

She would ask her to change a pumpkin in the garden into a magnificent carriage. She would ask her to change two mice into beautiful white horses. And she would ask her to take four lizards from the garden and change two of them into coachmen to drive the carriage and two of them into footmen to hold open the carriage door and help her in. Then she would go to the ball.

These thoughts made Cinderelma feel so good she began wishing very hard that a fairy godmother really would appear. But nothing happened. No matter how hard she wished, no fairy godmother came to her aid. Cinderelma then went to the window and wished upon her favorite star. "Please make a fairy godmother appear," she said. "Please!" Again, nothing happened. She stuck her head out the window and looked everywhere. But there was no fairy godmother to be seen.

Now Cinderelma was even sadder. "There's no such thing as a fairy godmother," she said and she threw herself on her bed and cried until she finally fell asleep. Later that night, Cinderelma was awakened by the happy laughter of her stepmother and stepsisters. They had just come home from the ball and Cinderelma could hear them talking.

"Oh, wasn't it wonderful," sighed the ugliest stepsister. "The Prince is so handsome and so rich!" "Did you see the way he looked into my eyes when he danced with me?" said the meanest stepsister.

"Tomorrow night I'm sure he will ask to marry me."

"No, he won't," shrieked the ugliest.

"Yes, he will!" screamed the meanest.

"You don't think he'd marry you, do you? You're too ugly!"

"Now girls," said the stepmother. "Stop fighting and go to bed. You must be as charming and beautiful tomorrow night as you were tonight."

As Cinderelma listened to her stepsisters talk she felt worse than ever. But the next day, instead of crying and wishing for a fairy godmother, she began to think of ways she could get to the ball. By evening she had a plan. That night, as soon as her stepmother and stepsisters had left for the ball, Cinderelma borrowed the meanest stepsister's most beautiful dress and put it on. She borrowed the ugliest stepsister's most magnificent wig. She borrowed some of her stepmother's best jewelry. Then, she got her ruby red ring from its secret place and put it on her finger. As she looked in the mirror, she could not believe how pretty she was.

Because she had no carriage, coachmen, or footmen Cinderelma had to walk to the palace. She crept along the street through the shadows to avoid being seen. Her heart was pounding with excitement. She was both scared and happy at the same time. As she walked up the palace stairs she held her head up high. The guards at the palace gate were so struck by her beauty they could barely speak.

When Cinderelma entered the grand ballroom, everyone wondered who she was. Even her stepmother and stepsisters didn't recognize her—though she was wearing their things.

"Who's that!" hissed the ugliest.

"I don't know," whispered the meanest, "but I'm sure the prince won't like her as much as he likes me." "He doesn't like you that much," shouted the ugliest.

"How would you know? You stupid, ugly thing!" yelled the meanest, and the two sisters began to fight.

Just then the Prince asked Cinderelma to dance and for the rest of the night he danced with no one else. He was enchanted by Cinderelma's beauty, her charm, and her grace. Who could this wonderful woman be?

Cinderelma was also delighted by the Prince. If only she could marry this marvelous man, all her problems would be over! But suddenly the clock struck twelve. Cinderelma knew she had to get home before her stepmother and stepsisters or else they would find out what she had done.

"I must leave now," said Cinderelma.

"Please," begged the Prince, "please stay longer."

"No, I can't," cried Cinderelma, "I must go home!"

Cinderelma pulled her hand away from the Prince and ran toward the palace door. But as she did so, her ruby red ring came off in the Prince's hand. "Don't go!" the Prince called but it was too late. Cinderelma had disappeared, leaving only her ring behind.

A few days later, the Prince announced that he would find and marry the owner of the ruby red ring. All the ladies of the kingdom were very excited. Each hoped the ring would fit her and she could claim to be its owner.

When the Prince's guards brought the ring to Cinderelma's house, the stepsisters couldn't wait to try it on. The meanest rubbed grease on her finger so the ring would slide on easily. The ugliest soaked her hand in cold water to make her finger thinner. But the ruby red ring didn't fit either of them. Their fingers were too big and too fat.

Suddenly one of the guards saw Cinderelma kneeling by the fireplace.

"Come here, young woman," he said. "You must try on this ring."

"Oh, don't bother with her," said the ugliest stepsister.

"She's just a wretched serving girl," said the meanest stepsister.

But the guard held out the ring and Cinderelma tried it on. You can imagine how astonished the stepsisters were when the ring fit perfectly.

"You horrible girl," cried the ugliest stepsister.

"My Prince," sobbed the meanest stepsister. "You stole my Prince!"

And so Cinderelma was brought to the palace. Both the Prince and Cinderelma cried with joy when they saw each other. The Prince said he wished to marry her and asked her to live at the palace while the court prepared for the royal wedding.

The following days were very happy for the Prince and Cinderelma. Every day they walked in the palace gardens and spoke of their love for each other. They made plans for their wonderful wedding. Kings and queens, princes and princesses, dukes and duchesses from all over the world were invited. It was very exciting and Cinderelma and the Prince never seemed to get tired of being with one another.

But when Cinderelma wasn't with the Prince, she wasn't very happy. She didn't enjoy the time she had to spend with the Queen and the other ladies of the court. They talked about all the things lords and ladies did. To her surprise, Cinderelma wasn't interested. She found talk about the court boring and stupid. And the things she liked talking about didn't interest the Queen and the other ladies. So instead of spending time with them, Cinderelma began to get to know the people who worked in the palace—people like the cooks, gardeners, coachmen, guards, and maidservants. She became especially friendly with the seamstress who made dresses and gowns for the ladies of the court. This woman liked Cinderelma and taught her how to make fine dresses. Cinderelma was a very good student and she learned very quickly.

One day the Queen told Cinderelma she should learn how to read, and play music, and draw. In those days, only the richest ladies of the kingdom knew how to do all these things and Cinderelma was thrilled by the idea. These were things she had always wanted to learn. And so, teachers were brought from a nearby university and each day Cinderelma spent many hours with them. She was a good student, worked very hard, and soon learned how to do all of these things.

Now Cinderelma and the Prince were spending even less time together. When they did see each other they found that they had less and less to talk about. The Prince was interested in hunting, fishing, and things that happened in the court. Cinderelma was much more interested in the dresses she was making and the books she was reading. Although the wedding was drawing closer, they didn't even talk very much about that any more.

One day the Prince said that he would have to be away for a few weeks. His father, the King, was sending him on business to a near-by country.

To her surprise, Cinderelma found that she didn't miss the Prince very much while he was away. She wanted to miss him but she didn't. So, when the Prince returned from his journey Cinderelma said, "I'm sorry I have to say this, but I no longer wish to marry you. We're different kinds of people and are interested in different things. I don't think we'd be very happy living together for the rest of our lives."

The Prince replied, "I have similar feelings and sadly I agree it would be best for us not to marry." Then he took Cinderelma's hand. "You have given me great moments of happiness, Cinderelma. I will always remember them and I thank you for them."

"You have given me fond memories too," said Cinderelma,"and because of you I have learned to paint, to play music, and to read. I can now make fine dresses and with this skill I can earn my own way. I never have to go back to my cruel stepmother and stepsisters. I am very grateful to you."

And so the next day the Prince and Cinderelma kissed each other good-bye and Cinderelma left the palace. Two of the Prince's servants went along with her to protect her on the journey. They left her at the town gate and waved good-bye.

In the town, Cinderelma had no trouble finding work as a seamstress. She worked long hours but enjoyed it. Soon she was admired for her skill.

During this time she saved her earnings until she finally had enough money to open her own dress shop in another part of the town.

Cinderelma was very proud of her shop. It was her very own and she had bought it with her own money. As time passed, she became more and more well known for the fine gowns she made. Many grand ladies came to buy her dresses. The store next to Cinderelma's was owned by a young printer. He, too, was a very hardworking man and he was well known for the fine work he did. In the evenings, after a hard day's work, he and Cinderelma would often talk together. He loved to read books and had never known anyone who read as well as she.

As time passed, Cinderelma and the printer got to know one another quite well. They did many enjoyable things together. They went horseback riding. They went to plays. And they danced at village festivals. They never seemed to get bored with one another. They never seemed to get tired of doing things together. In time, they married, and had children, and lived together until the end of their days. ❅

The Indian Cinderella
TRADITIONAL NATIVE AMERICAN STORY

❅ There once was an Algonquin hunter with magical powers. He could make himself invisible and listen in on people's conversations, schemes, and plans. Naturally, his powers made him very desirable, and many women wanted to marry him. At night, while sitting around the communal fire, they smiled at him hoping he would look their way. But he simply didn't notice them. When, in time, he decided to take a wife, he announced, "I will marry the first woman who can see me coming home at night, even though I am invisible."

Naturally, every woman wanted to win the heart of the hunter. But how? For no one could see him when he was invisible. No one, except his sister, who had the power to see her brother always.

One day, the hunter's sister said, "I think I know a way for you to find the kind of wife you are looking for." And she devised a clever test for all the women who sought her brother's hand in marriage. Each evening, at dusk, she would stroll with a different woman along the river's edge. When she would see her brother pass by, she would ask each woman, "Can you see him yet?"

"Oh yes!" they always answered, even though they couldn't see a thing. "Really?" the sister asked suspiciously. "Then tell me what he is wearing." The women would lie to her, of course, hoping to convince the sister that they could see her brother. "Uh, uh, a painted fabric." "A deerskin." "A beaded robe," they would answer. But the sister knew they weren't speaking the truth, since she could see her brother, and he was wearing bright feathers. And the warrior would only marry a truthful woman.

Now as it happened, there was an old man, a widower, who resided in the village with his three daughters. The youngest daughter was by far the prettiest, with smooth skin and sparkling eyes and thick jet-black hair, but she was prone to frequent illnesses. Despite her infirmities, her older sisters were jealous of her beauty and treated her horribly.

"You're ugly!" they shouted at her. "And stupid too!" They would sometimes burn her hands and feet with hot coals and smear her face with charcoal. Whenever their father would inquire about his youngest daughter's condition, his oldest daughters would blame the youngest child, saying, "It's all her fault! She never listens to us and gets too close to the fire and falls in."

The two older daughters each wanted to marry the hunter and tried to convince his sister of their powers. "Of course, I can see him," the oldest said as she and the hunter's sister strolled along the river's edge one night. "He's wearing a leather pouch over his arm." The hunter's sister knew she was lying since the hunter had left his pouch at home that day. "Of course, I can see him!" said the other daughter the next evening. "He is walking his horse by the river's edge." The sister knew she was lying too, since her brother had walked home that night alone.

Now the old man's youngest daughter also dreamed of marrying the hunter. So one night, when the stars were particularly vibrant in the sky, she walked with the hunter's sister along the river's edge. "Can you see him?" the sister asked her. "No, I can't," said the youngest daughter. And the sister was shocked because it was the first time any girl had given a truthful answer. The sister tried tricking her once more. "Are you *sure* you can't see him ?" she asked. "Why yes," the young maiden answered. "I *can* see him now. Oh, he's absolutely lovely to look at. He has such kind eyes and is so strong." "What is his bowstring made of?" the sister asked her. "The Milky Way," the youngest daughter replied. "And what is he using to pull his horse?" "A rainbow," she replied.

It was then that the hunter's sister understood what had happened. Because the girl had spoken the truth, the hunter had made himself visible. "I believe you," said the sister to the girl. "I am convinced that you saw my brother." And she took the young maiden to her home and cleaned her up and combed her long hair. Then she dressed her in the finest robes and placed jewels on her ears and neck, and painted her face and got her ready for the wedding. When the warrior arrived home that night, he sat next to his exquisite bride, and he called her his wife. And so she was.

And because the hunter loved his wife so much, he decided to punish her sisters for the years of cruelty they inflicted on his bride. One evening, while the mean sisters were outside their home, gathering wood for the fire, the warrior turned them into aspen trees. And their roots took hold, right on the spot they had been gathering wood, and they remained there ever since. To this very day, the aspen tree still quivers and shakes, afraid of the great hunter's power. ✹

BIBLIOGRAPHY OF FAVORITE
READ-ALOUD STORIES

While researching stories for this book, I chanced upon Susan Poke, a children's librarian in the Jefferson Market branch of the New York Public Library. She's been reading aloud to children for over twenty-two years. Her advice? "1. Have fun. 2. Know your child. 3. Allow him/her to make some of the book choices. 4. Share the books, and your enthusiasm for them, with your children's friends and their parents. I'm sure these sound like platitudes but they come from the heart." In addition to her unbridled enthusiasm for children's literature, experience has taught her a thing or two about what children like to hear. Here is a list of Susan's favorite read-aloud stories:

Prekindergarten and Toddlers

Brown, Margaret Wise, *Good Night, Moon* (New York: Harper & Row, 1947; reprint edition, HarperCollins, 1991).

Hughes, Shirley, *Rhymes for Annie Rose* (New York: Lothrop, Lee & Shepard, 1995).

Hutchins, Pat, *Titch* (New York: Macmillan, 1971; reprint edition, Simon & Schuster Children's, 1993).

Rankin, Joan, *Scaredy Cat* (New York: Margaret K. McElderry Books, 1996; reprint edition: Aladdin Paperbacks, 1999).

Rathmann, Peggy, *10 Minutes Till Bedtime* (New York: G. P. Putnam's Sons, 1998).

Shannon, David, *No, David!* (New York: Blue Sky Press, 1998).

Grades K–1

Cohen, Miriam, *When Will I Read?* (New York: Greenwillow Books, 1977; reprint edition, Bantam Doubleday Dell, 1996).

Hong, Lily T., *Two of Everything* (Morton Grove, Ill.: A. Whitman, 1993).

Sendak, Maurice, *Where the Wild Things Are* (New York: Harper & Row, 1963; reprint edition, HarperTrophy, 1988).

Shulevitz, Uri, *One Monday Morning* (New York: Scribner, 1967; reprint edition, Aladdin Books, 1986).

Slobodkina, Esphyr, *Caps for Sale: A Tale of a Peddlar, Some Monkeys, and Their Monkey Business* (New York: W. R. Scott, 1947; reprint edition, HarperTrophy, 1987).

Wells, Rosemary, *Bunny Money* (New York: Dial Books for Young Readers, 1997).

Zion, Gene, *No Roses for Harry* (New York: Harper, 1958; reprint edition, HarperTrophy, 1976).

Grades 1–2

Collicott, Sharleen, *Toestomper and the Caterpillars* (Boston: Houghton Mifflin, 1999).

Demi, *The Empty Pot* (New York: Henry Holt, 1990).

De Paola, Tomie, *Strega Nona* (Englewood Cliffs, N.J.: Prentice-Hall, 1975; reprint edition, Aladdin Paperbacks, 1988).

Kellogg, Steven, *Pinkerton, Behave!* (New York: Dial Press, 1979; reprint edition, Dial Books for Young Readers, 1993).

Noble, Trinka Hakes, *Meanwhile, Back at the Ranch* (New York: Dial Books for Young Readers, 1987; reprint edition, Puffin, 1992).

Rathmann, Peggy, *Officer Buckle and Gloria* (New York: Putnam's, 1995).

Seeger, Pete, *Abiyoyo* (New York: Macmillan, 1986; reprint edition, Aladdin Paperbacks, 1994).

Grades 3–4

Browne, Anthony, *Piggybook* (New York: Knopf, 1986).

Kimmel, Eric, *Anansi and the Moss-covered Rock* (New York: Holiday House, 1988).

McDermott, Gerald, *Zomo the Rabbit* (San Diego: Harcourt Brace Jovanovich, 1992; reprint edition, Voyager Picture Book, 1996).

Pinkwater, Daniel, *Tooth-Gnasher Superflash* (New York: Four Winds Press, 1981; reprint edition, Aladdin Paperbacks, 1990).

Willis, Jeanne, *Earthlets, as Explained by Professor Xargle* (New York: E. P. Dutton, 1988).

CHAPTER BOOKS

Cleary, Beverly, *Ramona the Pest* (New York: William Morrow, 1968; reprint edition, Camelot, 1996).

Dahl, Roald, *James and the Giant Peach* (New York: Knopf, 1961; reprint edition, Penguin, 1996).

Lewis, C. S., *The Lion, the Witch and the Wardrobe* (New York: Macmillan, 1950; reprint edition, HarperCollins, 1994).

Shannon, George, *Stories to Solve* (New York: Greenwillow Books, 1985; reprint edition, William Morrow, 1991).

Grades 5–6

Byars, Betsy Cromer, *The Pinballs* (New York: Harper & Row, 1977; reprint edition, HarperCollins, 1987).

Clearly, Beverly, *Dear Mr. Henshaw* (New York: Morrow, 1983; reprint edition, Avon, 1994).

Rowling, J. K., *Harry Potter and the Sorcerer's Stone* (New York: A. A. Levine Books, 1998; reprint edition, Scholastic, 1999).

Spinelli, Jerry, *Maniac McGee* (Boston: Little, Brown, 1990; reprint edition, HarperCollins, 1992).

White, E. B., *Charlotte's Web* (New York: Harper, 1952; reprint edition, Harper-Collins 1974).

4

Wizards, Lizards, and Blizzards

Creating Imaginary Stories

*Just as an individual who is deprived of dream time becomes
psychotic, a person robbed of imagination time during waking hours
becomes physically and spiritually numb.*
RICHARD STONE, *The Healing Art of Storytelling*

One of my first teaching experiences was at a nature center in
Massachusetts. Each week, bus loads of irrepressible city kids
would arrive for seven days of hiking, swimming, and nature study.
But on this particular occasion, the group I was asked to work with
was composed of physically disabled children in wheelchairs. Until
then, my workshops required physical movement—stretching,
walking, miming, and hiking—and I suddenly found myself in a
quandary. What should I do? I decided to ask them to move anyway, through their imaginations.

My first volunteer was a six-grade boy from New Jersey named
José. I asked him to close his eyes and imagine himself in a wonderful place. He shut his eyes and after a few seconds of passionate

concentration, he was ready. "Where are you?" I asked. "I'm in an amusement park," he answered. "And what do you see?" I continued. "Umm, I see rides and cotton candy and lots of kids running all around." "And what do you hear, José?" "I hear laughter and kids screaming on rides." "And what do you smell?" I asked. He paused for a long time and then said, "It's the scent . . . of fun." Another boy, with blond ringlets, rolled his wheelchair up to the center of the circle. "I'm in a karate class," he said. "And what do you taste?" I asked. "I taste discipline," he answered.

We continued to create imaginary scenarios, journeying in our minds from one fantastic setting to another. One by one, the children startled me with their moving pictures. One girl was running freely on a beach, picking up shells and building sand castles. Another was a princess, climbing the stone stairs to her castle tower. Their make-believe stories lifted them out of their present reality and let them travel to places I couldn't ever fathom. For a brief moment, we all believed that anything was possible.

No one felt let down when the exercise was over. On the contrary, they were elated. They had captained their own ship, rewritten their storylines, flexed their imaginative muscles, and were beaming with self-confidence.

The imagination is a gift of unspeakable magnitude, capable of changing our lives by allowing us to see possibilities in everything. It helps us become "unrealistic," a trait that is essential for greatness, since it allows us to dream the unimaginable. It's a confidence booster and the world's greatest toy. It costs nothing and comes with an unlimited warranty and batteries that never die. But it does need recharging.

Our imaginations, like the rest of our bodies, need exercise. By making up imaginary stories with your children, you'll exercise their creative muscles while giving your own mind a workout at the same time.

Reading a story to your kids is great. But making up a story is magical. It says so many things to your children. It tells them that it's okay to dream. It helps them to think outside the lines and form their own unique personalities. It gives them the chance to solve problems creatively. Best of all, it forges a beautiful bond between you and them.

Children's worlds are composed, in large part, of fantasy and imagination. By creating imaginary stories, you automatically enter their world, play on their turf, become "one of them," and this is extremely reassuring to children.

Even if you don't see yourself as an imaginative person and you fear your tales will be boring, make them up anyway. Inventing imaginary stories with your kids shouldn't be about results. It should be about the process of sharing and creating together. Who cares that your stories aren't works of literature? Certainly not your kids. They'll adore the attention you give them when you're sharing stories, one on one, or tailoring a story around them. The great thing about making up stories is that the more you do it, the easier it becomes and the more elaborate your stories get.

RECOGNIZING YOUR HIDDEN JEWELS

I like to begin my workshops by catching my participants off guard. During a recent session, I turned to a man in the circle and said, "Sir, it's a pleasure to have you in my session today. But was it necessary to wear a refrigerator on your head?" Initially he was stunned, but he recovered brilliantly by saying "Uh, yes, because I get hungry and I need to carry around food with me at all times."

"Open the refrigerator door, will you, sir, and take out something from inside it," I contrive.

"It's a banana," he says, playing along with my game.

"You've smuggled that banana into this room from your exotic and foreign country haven't you, sir?" I ask. "Tell us who you really are and why you smuggled it in."

Now, he starts to get a naughty look on his face, and he begins to really have fun. "Okay, you found me out," he answers." I'm the king of a faraway land and we have everything there except bananas. I was bringing this one home so that I could sell it for a lot of money."

"Your sister told me that you're here for another reason altogether," I say, turning to the women sitting to his left. "Reach into his refrigerator and pull out an object."

The women to his left is also taken off guard and doesn't know what to do at first. But slowly, she reaches over his head and pretends to be fishing around in a refrigerator, before pulling out a long, stringy object.

"It's lace," she says. "Yards of lace." She mimes pulling and pulling on the never-ending ball of lace until finally I instruct a woman sitting across the room to cut it.

"Now, tell us what happened with your brother and that lace, " I say to her.

Without missing a beat, she says, "Last night, I caught my brother using this long piece of lace to climb up a banana tree. He was about to pluck six more bananas when I shouted, 'Stop! You'll get arrested if anyone catches you!' "

"But your shouts were so noisy, they alerted the police who did come after your brother, correct?" I ask her.

"Yes," she says.

Now I ask a man to her left to read the invisible word hanging on the bottom of the lace.

"Button," he says.

"Mr. Policeman, " I say to him. "What happened with that button when you arrived at the scene of the crime?"

"Well, I was awakened by her screams and I threw on my pants in a hurry, but I must have been half-asleep because I forgot to button them and they fell down in the middle of a busy street. It was humiliating." We burst into laughter.

I remind my group that they created a tale from absolutely nothing. No books. No script. No props. No pictures. Just an invisible refrigerator and their wacky inner musings. They're exhilarated.

When I run workshops, I always begin with the supposition that everyone is like a safe-deposit box, possessing a storehouse of unimaginable riches. I truly believe that each of us has a resplendent imagination. It may be hiding behind layers of literal thinking, but it's there. Because I have such faith in our innate imaginations, I'm convinced that anyone can easily learn how to tell fabulous make-believe stories.

Obviously, children need very little prompting. Their imaginations are vivid and abundant, and with little direction they're able to tell ingenious stories. The real problem, unfortunately, is with us, the grown-ups. We are the models for our kids. If we fail to see the imaginative possibilities in everything, so will our kids. It's up to us to encourage and welcome imaginary stories into our home.

I'm concerned with the cynicism I see in young people at an increasingly early age. I recently performed at a birthday party for four-year-olds. When I carried an imaginary box into the room, at least three kids shouted, "That's not real." Of course, once I asked them to fish something out of the box and describe it, they fully participated. At four, they had already learned to see things concretely. But given the chance to reverse that process, they grabbed it. Which leads me to believe that as much as we'd like to ascribe the ailing imaginations of our children to television and the Internet, the culprit probably lies closer to home, with us, their models. We need to let our kids know that it's okay to take flights of fancy by taking them ourselves.

Part of our inhibitions stem from the pressure we feel to come up with "the goods." How can our stories compete with a Spielberg or a Disney film? They can't, and they shouldn't. I've mentioned this point throughout the book, but it's worth mentioning again: Your focus should be on the creative process, not the story. Even if you don't complete an imaginary story, or even if it's just plain bad, it really doesn't matter. Your kids will have a chance later on in life to produce a polished novel or a screenplay. For now, we're laying the foundation for their thinking and giving them a priceless gift: the belief that it's okay to dream, to imagine.

ONCE UPON A TIME . . .

Aristotle came up with the idea over 2,000 years go. It must have been a good one because we've been following his lead ever since. He said that the basic elements of a story include a beginning, a middle, and an end. Let's look at how we can apply that to our own stories.

The Beginning

The beginning of a story is an invitation. It beckons you to listen by setting the stage for the impending story: "Once upon a time. . . ." "A long time ago. . . ." "In a small village, far, far away, there lived a princess." It also lays out information. "In a land far away, there was a man who lived alone in an abandoned castle. He had lived there for many years in total solitude, and he liked it that way."

The Middle

The middle needs to include a problem, a conflict. If there's no problem, your story will fall flat. "One day a young man showed up at the front door of the castle with a deed in his hand. 'This was my family's home over a hundred years ago,' said the visitor. 'It was stolen away during the war. I believe this castle rightfully belongs to me.' 'What?!' said the king, horrified. 'But because you've been here so long, I'll let you stay,' said the boy. 'We'll both live here!' "

The End

The end resolves the conflict, either through confronting it head on or by avoiding it, and finds closure to the story. " 'What?!' said the king. 'Unthinkable!!!!!!!' He huffed and puffed and stormed through the castle. He bolted the front door and boarded up the windows. He turned out the lights and shut off his phone. He waited for twenty years before he opened that front door again. And when he did, he saw a young man walking up the path to his castle. 'Hello, sir! My father's father left me the deed to this castle in his will. Apparently, it belongs to my family. . . .' "

CREATING A STORY

One of the easiest tales to create is a *sequence story*, which traces your day sequentially. We'll use an ordinary task—going to the grocery store—as our subject matter.

Let's break down the elements of your journey to the grocery store:

The beginning or setup: You needed groceries since there were none left in the house. You knew your kids were coming home from school by 3 P.M., and you had to get to the store before they got home because neither of your kids has a key to your front door and it's the middle of winter.

The middle or conflict: You're about to leave your house for the grocery store when the phone rings. You get detained on the phone for fifteen minutes and by the time you leave for the grocery store, it's already 2:30. You figure you'll shop quickly and be home in time for your kids, but unbeknownst to you, trouble is brewing at the store. The woman in front of you in the check-out line has three hundred coupons, which take endless amounts of time to sort. You're stuck in the line, there are ten people in front of you, and all the other registers are filled up with people, too. So you wait. It's now 2:50. It's now 3:10. By the time you finish, it's 3:30. You hope the kids went next door to the neighbor's house.

The end or resolution: Now it's time to resolve the conflict. You arrive home and see your kids waiting on the front stoop outside your home. But you notice your kids look sick. Their hands and tongue have turned purple. "Oh my god! What happened?! You must have caught pneumonia!" Frantically you get them inside and put them in front of the radiator to heat up. But they begin to giggle and as they laugh, their pockets bulge. Purple wads of gum come tumbling out onto the floor. "So that's why you're purple!" you say, at first with relief and then with frustration. "I went shopping so I could make a big dinner and now you've spoiled your appetite!"

That's our first draft. Now let's add some spice to the story by using some advice I picked up from the writer Kurt Vonnegut during a radio interview he gave. When asked if he had any suggestions for aspiring writers, he said, "Make sure you write in a dreadful character, the one everyone hates who's always doing something nasty to someone. That way your nice characters will have someone to react to."

Using his advice, let's bring in a dreadful character. But remember, you always must establish who the central character is and what her mission is up front; otherwise you'll lose your audience.

Beginning: "I knew I shouldn't have answered the phone when it rang. I only had thirty minutes to get to the grocery store and back before my kids got home from school. I tried to explain to my sister Shirley that I couldn't talk, but she relentlessly kept yapping and yapping away. By the time I unhinged my ear from the phone it was already 2:45. With fifteen minutes to spare, I raced off to the grocery store.

Middle: Things might have gone smoothly were it not for the shrew in front of me at the check-out counter. Old Mrs. Pretzl-wetzel, the miserly old woman from Jackson Street whose coupon collection is so large that there's no room to walk into her house anymore, was standing in front of me. What could I do? I twiddled my thumbs. I sighed and complained to the woman in line behind me. "I heard that!" Mrs. Pretzlwetzel said. "You better watch it, Missy, or I'll put a curse on you and those rotten kids of yours!"

"How dare you say nasty things about my kids?" I said to her, and bopped her on the head with my purse. Somehow my purse pulled off her wig and that really started things in motion. Mrs. Pretzlwetzel slid across the room on her wig, like a surfboard, landing in the cheese bin.

End: Now it's time for you and your kids to end this story, using the first draft as your guide. Feel free to add some spice and curves to the story, but remember to resolve the narrator's initial problem: getting home in time to let the kids inside the house. Make sure you create an ending spontaneously by *telling* it to one another, not by *writing* it down first.

Piecing Together the Elements

Pick a word from each of the categories in the table. Create a story combining all of your selections.

PERSON	PLACE	CONFLICT
A dinosaur	Texas	Finds stolen goods
Batman	A soccer field	Is being chased
A little girl	A pick-up truck	Got fired from job
A little boy	The seashore	Turned into a frog
Frank, a teenager	The forest	Is lost
A hot-dog vendor	A movie theater	Knows a secret

SOLVING THE PROBLEM	ENDING THE STORY
Waves a magic wand	Returns home having learned a lesson
Uses a compass	Changes into something else
Discovers a hidden talent	Receives a great gift
Phones for help	Becomes wiser
Metamorphoses into	Finds peace

Dialogue It!

One of the ways to make any story better is by adding dialogue, even in places where it seems impossible to do so. Let's look at the following sentence: "Once upon a time, a little girl with long red hair walked to school, passing the pharmacy, the ice cream store, and the fire station along the way."

To add dialogue, try breaking up your sentences to create hidden opportunities. If I were telling this story, I might say, "Once upon a time, a little girl with long red hair walked to school, passing the pharmacy. 'Hello, Mr. Smith!' she shouted to the silver-haired pharmacist, whose handlebar mustache danced up and down when he spoke. Then she passed the ice cream store. 'Hello, ice cream cones!' she said to her favorite, mint chocolate chip ice cream, which she ate sometimes after school. She passed the fire station too. 'Hello, fire truck!' she called out to the long red hook and ladder. But to her surprise, it answered back."

With your children, try adding dialogue to the following simple sentences. Don't cheat by completely changing the plot. Try to stay within the framework of the existing sentence. You can embellish with details, but don't change the overall plot. Remember, trees, flowers, animals, or any inanimate objects are potential conversationalists.

1. One day, Mr. Smith opened his front door and found that there were two newspapers instead of one.
2. As Jason walked down the block to his friend Peter's house, the sky turned dark and the wind began to swirl in huge gusts.
3. It was time to pick you guys up from camp, so I got into my car and began to drive along the road I always take.

Using Similes

Similes can help you develop richer, more descriptive language in your stories. Instead of saying, "It was dark outside," wouldn't it be more captivating to say, "It was so dark outside that the sky turned black as molasses." To get you and your kids thinking more descriptively, complete the following similes:

1. She was so short that she looked like_____.
2. The sun was as bright as_____.
3. Her hair was as red as_____.
4. She was as hungry as_____.

Sense It!

One of the most common mistakes among beginning storytellers is their reliance on visual descriptions at the exclusion of the other senses. "She wore a red scarf" is a nice description, but "Her red scarf was so itchy it made her scratch her neck from morning to night" adds a new dimension.

Try adding a description to the following sentences that includes a sound, touch, smell, or taste.

1. The dog came into the house covered in mud_____.
2. My hamburger looked disgusting_____.
3. Santa Claus looked funny when he landed in my fireplace____.
4. The fire was ablaze by the time the firemen arrived _____.

Make It Colorful. One of the ways you'll improve your storytelling abilities dramatically is by widening your storehouse of adjectives. Choose a simple object, like a business card. Pass it around in a circle and take turns describing the object with a different one-word adjective. It's important to stick to one word only, as it will force you to come up with new ways of seeing an object. When you think you've run out of words, keep going! That's when the real creative thinking begins. You'll have to reach in the back of your brain for nonvisual descriptions, like "scentless" or "silky." This activity will strengthen not only your imagination, but your vocabulary as well.

STORIES THAT SOOTHE

When I was little, I was bilingual. My first language was English. My second was Mommy-tongue. It sounded something like this. "Mommy! I'm thirsty!" Translated, it meant, "I'm afraid. Can you stay with me in my room for a while?" My mother also spoke Mommy-tongue fluently and would climb under the covers and cuddle next to me, and after a few moments, she would dispense the appropriate medicine: a story. For some reason, she always sang her stories instead of speaking them. That was part of the fun, because her voice was absolutely dreadful and it always cracked both of us up. "There once was a little girl," she would sing, "who had a little curl, and wore it in a swirl (now she would change melodies entirely), she was so afraid of everything around, including the wet ground. . . ." Her lyrics had to rhyme and they were so ridiculous that the two of us couldn't help but laugh hysterically. In her songs, the central character was always me. She would tackle my childhood fears by integrating them into her outrageous plots, where I would stand up to a lion, fight a group of local bullies, defend my brother. But they worked. They calmed me and I was able to sleep through the night. But they did more than alleviate my insomnia. They endowed me with a belief that I could author my own stories and rewrite my character. They also gave me a place to work out many of my fears. Best of all, they united me in a beautiful bond with my mother. These were our most intimate moments together, creating stories out of thin air, fueled by imagination and love.

Children often have a hard time talking about their problems. Sometimes, they're not even capable of identifying what they are anxious about. Creating stories in which you feature your children and their surroundings can help them deal with issues that are troubling them, and can allow them to learn about themselves in a safe way that makes them feel understood and supported. They also enable children to be the heroes of their worlds, and reinforce day-to-day experiences.

When my niece Molly was three years old, she stepped on a nail. She had to go to the hospital to have it removed, and it was pretty traumatic for her. For months after that, she kept wanting to hear the story of "Molly and the Nail." My sister and I kept telling her the story over and over. . . . "One day, you were playing in the yard when suddenly you started screaming. So I ran over and picked you up and you were crying. . . ." I describe the ambulance ride and how brave she was, the doctors at the hospital, and bringing her home. Retelling the incident as a story helped her process what had happened to her. It also somehow made it more distant for her, so she could be the heroine of the story as opposed to the victim. I think it was her way of conquering the fear.

LYNN ANN KLOTZ, aunt of Molly, 6

In the *Yarnspinner*, a storytelling journal, Judith Black, a professional Boston-area storyteller (and one of my favorites), described the benefits of using her home-spun character, Solouse the Mouse, in the original stories she wove for her son, Solomon, throughout his childhood.

Solouse is different enough from Solomon that the mouse can live out situations that my son can't. Whether riding a bike or going on an airplane, Solouse dares and fails and tries again, and Solomon gains strength from him. But the modeling isn't just from parent to child. Solomon suggests feelings, situations, and results that enable me to understand him better. In "Solouse the Mouse Goes to Visit His Uncle John," the mouse fought with a huge cat that stood at the turnpike entrance, grabbed the mouse cars, ripped them open like sardine cans with one powerful claw and gobbled them down. The cat was extraordinarily vivid and when it came time to do battle, my son suggested, "Mama, I think Solouse should trick the cat and sneak all the other mice away." The image had gone too far for him, and he let me know what he needed. Through the stories, we cross boundaries and share secrets that we might not have otherwise.

The following abridged excerpt is from *Annie Stories*, a book of original tales created by Doris Brett, a clinical psychologist from Australia, for her daughter, Annie. Although clearly influenced by her psychology background, the following passage, from a story about childhood nightmares, may spawn some ideas for creating a soothing story of your own.

Annie was a little girl who lived in a brown brick house with her mommy and daddy and a big black dog. . . .[1] One of the things Annie liked best about her room was her bed. It was white and red, and underneath it were two big drawers that Annie kept her toys in.

Sometimes Annie had good dreams and she would wake up feeling happy. Sometimes, though, she had bad dreams and she would wake up feeling frightened. When that happened she would turn on the little light next to her bed and get one of her books and look at the pictures or read.[2]

One night Annie had a very scary dream. She dreamed that she was being chased by wild animals. She ran and ran but she could hear the animals thundering behind her. They were getting closer and closer. She could hear them panting and feel their hot breath through the back of her dress. All of a sudden, just as they were about to snap their big, nasty, teeth down on her, she woke up. She went to find her mother to tell her about her terrible dream.

Annie's mother comforts her child and gives her an invisible magic dream ring that, she tells her, will protect her from harm. She also tells Annie that she has the power to alter events in her dreams. "All you need to do is remember in your dreams that you can change it, and then you can make whatever you like happen," she says.

Most of us don't have Ms. Brett's training. Yet even if you don't have a psychology degree, common sense and instinct will guide you in inventing your own soothing story. It needn't be about a problem in your child's life. Your story can reinforce small victories,

1.Vary the details here to fit in with your child's environment.
2. A night light or lamp next to the bed is very reassuring for children.

like learning how to ride a bike, catching a baseball for the first time, or playing a song on the piano.

> Lately, I've been creating fireman stories with my son, who is four. Naturally, he insists on being the captain of the hook-and-ladder truck. He always ends up rescuing Isaiah, this older boy who lives in the neighborhood. Now in real life, Isaiah is a very talented, very athletic boy, and I think my son feels a bit intimidated by him. So every character who either gets into trouble or is in need of saving he names Isaiah. I think it's my son's way of working out the competition.
>
> JEFF Y.

CREATION STORIES

Years ago, I received a grant to run a series of storytelling workshops on the Lower East Side of Manhattan with "at-risk" eight- and nine-year-olds. Every culture has a creation story of some kind, and so I decided to experiment with that type of story in this setting. After reading aloud stories from a variety of cultures, from ancient Greek, to Native American, to Eastern European, I asked my students to create their own tales entitled, "How the Sun Came to Be." The results were enchanting. These children, who were acutely aware of their label, which identified them as students at risk of failing or dropping out, flourished when given the opportunity to tax their imaginations while being the center of attention.

Everyone wanted their shot at making a creation story. The key was to have them *tell* their stories, not *write* them. For many children, writing a story implies judgment: Their spelling will be corrected, their grammar will be criticized, their penmanship will be scrutinized. Once they felt free to tap into their story ideas without being judged, they met the challenge head on. Here are a few of my favorites:

One day there was a person named The Sun. He was round all over. One day he found a fruit and ate it. When he opened his mouth, bright light came out. And from that day on, his mouth stayed open.

SAMMY

One day the sun was resting in the sky, when all of a sudden, a spaceship came down. The door opened. A big, hairy, repulsive creature came out. The creature had a laser gun in his hand. The creature shot the sun. There stood the sun glistening in the sky. And that's how the sun got its shine.

JUSTIN

A long time ago the sun and the moon happily lived together in the sky. One day the sun said to the moon, "I bet that I can be very bright and you can't." Now the moon was infuriated by the sun. But he still had a chance of winning, for at this time the sun was not very shining. "O.K.!" said the moon. "The bet is on. I'll see you at dusk tomorrow." "Oh, by the way," the sun said, "the winner gets a pot of gold." At dusk, the moon and the sun met. The sun won the contest and got the pot of gold. And until this day the sun is very radiant and the moon is very dark.

ARIELLE

Creation Elation. Now it's time for you and your children to come up with your own creation stories. Tell the story of

1. How the ocean came to be
2. How the sun came to be
3. How the moon came to be

Don't make this a writing assignment. Simply tell these stories spontaneously. You can always write them down later.

The story my kids love the best is the one I created about their magic journey across the seas. I'll say, "There once was a little girl named Rachel (my daughter) and a boy named Jacob (my son). When they were old enough to travel by themselves, they decided to take a boat trip together to visit different islands. When they arrived at the first island, though, it was like nowhere they had ever seen. You see, everything on the island was red! The women wore only red clothes and had red hair. They only grew tomatoes and apples and beets and you could only get strawberry chocolate milk." Then I make up three other islands with something equally odd on each one. For example, on one island everyone has three ears; on another everyone sings instead of talks. I usually ask them how life would be different if they lived on these islands. A lot of times, my kids will decide what kind of island it is. They absolutely love this game, since it has everything in it—silliness, problem solving, and imagination.

GISELLE BROWN, mother of Rachel, 4, and Jacob, 6

HOW TO PROMPT A STORY

Still having trouble coming up with your own story? Try prompting a story with the following activities.

Pass the Story. Start to tell a story and suddenly freeze. Point to a family member, who must continue the story immediately.

Rabbit Tales. Pull an imaginary rabbit out of a hat. Describe what it's wearing, thinking, and feeling. Was it working for a magician or simply napping in a cozy place? Share its story with other family members.

Where's 007? Take a secret message out of your ear and read it aloud. Perhaps it's a lengthy paragraph or maybe it's a simple sentence. Don't force yourself to be clever. Just read whatever pops into your imagination, even if it's only one word. Explain the story behind the message.

Furniture Folly. Everyone knows that to a lamp, its shade is its hat. Some lamps take great pride in their shades, showing them off whenever they can. Others are more casual about their shades. Find a table lamp in your house and study it for a few minutes. Tell the story of how the lamp shopped for its shade. Did it try on many different ones before settling on this one? Was it a snobby lamp who insisted on a high-class shade? Did other lamps fight for the same shade? Does a lamp change its shade according to the season or is it stuck with it for life?

Do the same thing with other pieces of furniture around your house. Windows shop for their drapes. A bed shops for its bedspread. Tell their stories.

The Invisible Man. Take turns introducing yourself and your invisible companion. Then explain why he is invisible. Is it intentional? Was there a magic potion he accidentally ingested? Or is he simply shy? Tell everyone the full story behind your friend's disappearing act.

Phoney Book. Take turns picking out interesting names in the phone book. Tell the life stories of the persons you've selected. Expand the activity by creating stories of two characters, also inspired by names in the phone book.

Paper Trail. On separate strips of paper write the names of places (Miami, the museum), people (grandpa, Bugs Bunny), and hobbies or habits (bowling, biting your nails), and place them in three separate hats, grouped by their categories. Then ask each family member to take out one strip of paper from each hat and create a story out of the three words.

City Ditty. Look on a map and find a city with an unusual or silly name. Create a story about that town and how it got its name.

When the professional storyteller Nancy Schimmel passed a turnoff to the town of Crossnore, as she drove along the Blue Ridge Parkway with her friend, Heather Crawan, on her way to the National Storytelling Festival in Tennessee, she began to wonder what a "crossnore" was. This story is her answer.

A Story for Heather
from *Just Enough to Make a Story*

❊ Once there was a little girl named Heather. Every morning she drove the goats to pasture, through the valley and up the hillside to the meadow, and every evening she drove them home again. As she walked along behind the goats, she always sang, songs she learned from her mother and father and songs she made up herself. In the morning she sang because she was happy and rested and ready for anything. In the evening she sang because a song is good company when you're alone with the goats and the shadows.

What Heather didn't know was that every day, as she walked through the valley, she walked right over a crossnore that lived under the ground—or rather I should say lived in the ground, for a crossnore moves through the ground like a shark through the sea or a tiger through the jungle. What they look like, nobody knows, for they never come out of the ground. This crossnore never moved far, though he wondered if the next valley might be better than his. He was always wanting to find out, but always wanting to get a good long sleep before he started, so he would be rested and ready for anything. And some meadowlark or thrush by day, some nightingale or melodious frog by night, was always waking him up in the middle of his good long sleep. Crossnores hate music. It always wakes them up, and the prettier the song, the more it wakes them up.

And the most annoying times in this crossnore's whole day were when he heard the trip-trap of the goats' hoofs (which he didn't mind at all) and then Heather's high, clear voice singing some beautiful song (which he minded awfully). He longed to grab Heather by her little bare toes and drag her into the ground and stop up her mouth with dirt, but her voice was so clear and sweet that he couldn't bear to get close enough to do it. So he bided his time, and grumbled.

Then one day, the goats passed overhead, and the pad-pad-pad of little bare feet, but the crossnore did not hear any singing. Heather had a cold and could not sing a note. In the morning, the crossnore was too surprised to catch her, but all day long, as he muttered at thrushes and shouldered sharp stones out of his bed, he plotted and planned to grab Heather's little bare toes and drag her under the ground that very night.

And all day long, Heather thought how lonely it would be, walking home through the evening shadows without a song for company. In the evening, when she started down the path, she still couldn't sing. At the head of the valley, she passed a clump of willows. She took out her knife and snicked off a piece of willow as she went by, and started to whittle as she walked. And as she walked, the crossnore waited, and listened, and soon he heard the trip-trap of the goats' hoofs, and the pad-pad-pad of Heather's little bare feet, but just as he grabbed for her little bare toes, she raised her new-made willow whistle to her lips and blew the clearest, sweetest tune the crossnore had ever heard. He dove straight down into the earth so fast the ground sank three feet right under Heather, and Heather sank with it. She climbed out of the hole and whistled her way home, and the crossnore moved to the next valley and never came back.

When Heather got home, she told her mother and father what had happened to her. They told her a nice story about underground streams and sinkholes, and she almost believed it, but she really won't know what happened until she hears the story of How Heather Whistled Away the Crossnore. ❀

5

Gobble Your Goblins

Taking the Scare out of Ghost Stories

My first professional job should have been my last. It was October 31, and I had been hired by a history museum to tell New York ghost stories to a family audience. I had put together what I believed was a fabulous Halloween program of legends and folklore which revealed the historical apparitions and goblins that purportedly still haunt the Big Apple—the "rap tap tapping" of Peter Stuyvesant's wooden leg, the milky white apparition of the ghost of Captain Kidd, the ghoulish outline of the storm ship that appears in the Hudson River after a heavy rain—a program I had spent six months researching and practicing.

Things started out fine. I began my story, and the toothless boy directly in front of me giggled. A great sign. The blond kid to his left follows with a belly laugh. So far so good. Now, for the clincher, I recreate the loud screech of an old wooden doorway. A four-year-old bursts into tears. Her mother scoops her up and leaves. No harm yet. I continue, recreating the shrill witch's chant around a smoking cauldron and the "Boom!" of an unexpected goblin. Child number two starts bawling his eyes out. The three-year-old in front of him joins in. Their parents do nothing, and three more infants join the chorus of wailers. It's a baby shower, literally. Concentrate and keep going, I say to myself, as I continue to describe Henry Hudson's lost ship to my distracted listeners. But I know my storyboat is about to become shipwrecked. Pandemonium has broken loose. Now parents in the audience begin to fly out of that auditorium. I'm mortified. By the time the mass exodus ends, only four children are left in the room. And one very humiliated storyteller knows she'll be haunted by this performance long after Halloween is over.

What went wrong? Well, for starters, the children in my audience were too young for my material. Even though the museum had asked me to gear my tales for older kids, I should have adapted my stories to my audience. I also didn't have enough experience to know that when kids ask for scary stories, they don't always mean what they say.

Children like to pretend they're a lot tougher than they really are. But if we aren't careful, what seems like a harmless ghost story can give children nightmares for weeks. That's because young children's ability to distinguish between make-believe and real isn't fully developed. In addition, their imagination is infinite and can conjure up images that may be far more frightening than those from a story on television and that can stay with children for a long time. Therefore, it's important that parents take some control over the ghost stories that are told around the house, tempering frightening images in a storybook and adjusting the story as you read aloud.

That's not to say that I believe all scary stories are bad. On the contrary, many children work out their fears and anxieties by hearing scary stories. They are able to watch someone else combat villains and evil forces, from the safety of their own home. All children are individuals and as such, react in their own unique way to any given story. As their parents, you'll have to gauge their "fright quotient" and choose your stories accordingly. Because we're exposed to scary images frequently, through television, film, or the Internet, it's easy to forget how quickly young children can become rattled.

Since my first performance debacle at the museum, I've learned a few things about how to bring the spirit of Halloween to life, without the fright. For starters, it's not necessary to choose a scary story. Remember, small children will be just as captivated by silly ghosts and whimsical apparitions as they will be by frightening ones. Making your ghost story come alive depends less on its content and more on its delivery. In cartoons, characters fall off cliffs, get run over by three-thousand-pound boulders, and break up into a thousand pieces. Yet, we find them funny, not scary. That's because cartoons use humor to portray what would otherwise be very scary scenarios. Do the same when you are reading a ghost story to your child. Be funny. Substitute silly voices for frightening ones, or exaggerated movements for threatening ones.

Nowadays when I'm hired to tell ghost stories, I'm much more careful about the stories I choose. Rather than telling a frightening story, I've learned to create suspenseful moments out of nonthreatening text through pauses, whispers, and facial expressions. I've learned to gauge the receptivity of my audience through instinct, not through some hard-and-fast rule about age appropriateness. Each child's tolerance level is different, depending on his or her experience and temperament. But I believe it's better to err on the side of caution, testing the waters slowly by modifying scary tales.

While older children may boast about their ability to withstand horror stories, don't be fooled. Even children in their early teens can frighten easily. One of the best ways to engage older kids without actually scaring them is to have them create their own ghost stories. Children need to feel that they are in control of their world, and creating original stories can help them do just that. You can also create a story in which children get to speak to the monster or ghoul that's frightened them. Sometimes by confronting our demons we take away their power to scare us.

Most professional storytellers develop their own techniques for combating fear among their audience members. When Robin Moore tells scary stories, he starts his programs by saying, "If you're the type of kid who has bad dreams, tonight, when you go to bed, place your shoes in opposite directions from one another in front of your bed," a device that, he contends, keeps ghosts and ghouls at bay. Tim Jennings tells his favorite ghost story to kids from the perspective of a young boy. "Kids became scared to death when I told them this story," he says. "Somehow, when a grown-up tells a ghost story and revels in its gory details, it seems icky and frightening. Now I tell the same story as a little boy and the kids have no problem whatsoever."

There used to be an old man who came to our house named Hall. I would hear people say, "Mr. Hall wears a rug." I didn't know what a rug was. I'd lay down on the floor and Grandma would say, "What are you doing?" "I'm trying to find Mr. Hall's rug." And Grandma would say, "Get up, get up! That ain't nice." Well one day Mr. Hall was there and Grandpa started into one of his scary stories. There was a piece of wood burning in the fireplace, sort of sticking out, and Pa spotted it. I watched him put his tobacco way back in his mouth so that he could get a good long shot. At just the right moment in the story, he threw his head forward and that tobacco came out and hit that wood just right; it fell off on the floor and the fire sparked up. Somebody threw a baby on the floor, men ran out, and Mr. Hall ran out too. When he passed us, Mr. Hall's scalp was as naked as the palm of my hand. Jesus have mercy! Granddaddy scared the rug right off Mr. Hall's head! Well, I went over to his chair, and there in Mr. Hall's hat was his scalp! I picked it up. "Grandma! Is this Mr. Hall's rug?" Grandma said, "Put that thing down and go wash your hands." Oh, I loved those days when Grandpa told his scary stories.

JACKIE TORRENCE, *Jackie Tales*

HOW TO HAVE FUN WITH SCARY STORIES

1. Choose your stories wisely. Don't overestimate your child's capacity to handle a scary story, no matter how "cool" he says he is. Look for stories that are playful, not frightening, mysterious, not violent. Avoid stories in which a character gets killed or dismembered. Keep in mind that a story can still be scary and suspenseful without having to result in violence or death.

2. Substitute humor for horror. Make frightening characters into cartoon-like figures. Instead of a headless horseman, make him a horseman with a marshmallow for a head. If your story features an evil, knife-wielding pirate, transform him into a buccaneer who threatens his victims by making them drink a gallon of chocolate milk as they walk down the gangplank. Remember, jolly villains can be just as riveting as gruesome ones.

3. Whisper, don't shout. Loud voices can easily rattle small children and aren't necessary to create suspense in a story. You can captivate your listeners just as easily by lowering rather than raising your voice. Even if your story calls for a loud noise, like a scream, the slamming of a door, or the loud thump of a character's foot, try whispering it instead of shouting it. The children will be more compelled to listen, and you'll save your voice in the process.

4. Modulate your voice. You can create suspense in *any* story by the way you tell it. Try choosing a silly rather than frightening story, and give it a Halloween flavor by embellishing it with eerie sound effects, whispers, or moans. Remember, it's always easier to start with a nonthreatening story and add suspense to it, than having to compensate for a story that's too frightening.

One of the best ways to take the scare out of a story is by making your delivery humorous. Remember, you can alter the feeling of any line in a story by changing dialects, adding gestures, modulating your voice, or using comical facial expressions. You can also bring out the humor in a line by creating a visual picture of an image that is the opposite of its description. For example, while you are reading a passage in a book that says, "She was tall," stick your nose to the ground and mumble, "Oh, there she is!" You'll extract giggles from your kids simply by your opposite interpretation of the material.

Try making the following sentences funny:

a. The vampire walked into the room, his fangs dangling, and said, "You're looking very beautiful indeed, young lady."

b. She thought she was alone in the cemetery. But suddenly, she felt a warm gust of wind swirling around her and a little finger running up and down her spine. She knew she wasn't the only one there.

c. The witch's brew was complete. With one swirl of her broomstick in the hot, steaming concoction, the mean witch said to the young maiden, "Now, I'll turn you into a goat."

5. Don't show graphic illustrations. A visual image can stay with children for years, particularly if the picture is a frightening one. If the illustration in your story book is too disturbing, resist showing it to your children. Instead, have them use their imaginations to create their own images. Ask them to describe what the characters look like or have them draw pictures of the characters.

SPOOKY ACTIVITIES WITHOUT THE FRIGHT

Tell Jokes. Instead of a scary story, try telling your kids a joke:

Why did the invisible man look in the mirror?
To see if he wasn't there.

What do birds say on Halloween?
Twick or tweet!

Why do skeletons drink a lot of milk?
Because it is good for their bones.

What did the ghost say when he got scared?
I want my mummy.

What is the first thing ghosts do when they get into a car?
They fasten their sheet (seat) belts.

What kind of test does a vampire take in school?
A blood test.

Add Dialogue. One of the best ways to counterbalance a scary passage is by adding funny dialogue to it. If a ghost rises from a tombstone and starts blowing around, add a few lines like, "What does a ghost have to do around here to get some attention? When I worked at the mall, everyone used to run for cover the minute I rose from the clothes racks. I've got to get a new gig."

After reading the following passage from "The Coming of the Demon" in *The Haunted South* by Nancy Roberts, create dialogue with your kids.

The Livingstones were in bed listening to the rain and wind outside when they heard a pounding on the front door. Adam went down to see who it could be. He cautiously opened the door a few inches but the force of the wind was such that it tore the door from his hand and flung it open, revealing a black hole in the outer darkness. In the midst of it stood a tall stranger, his cloak billowing in the wind.

CREATING FRIENDLY GHOST STORIES

Friendly ghosts are appealing and nonthreatening to small children, and creating a story about them can be a wonderful way to welcome in the spirit of Halloween. Begin a tale about a friendly ghost and pass it to each member of the family, allowing the last person to end it.

Try the following games to help you create friendly ghost stories:

Frozen Monster. Tell a friendly ghost story. It can be either one you know or one you invent. Ask your kids to dance until you stop spinning your tale. Once you stop, they must freeze in the shape of a ghost. Whoever moves is eliminated from the game. The winner then becomes the storyteller in the next round.

Pumpkin Lore. Fill a plastic pumpkin with Halloween-related objects, such as candy, a witch's hat, or a Halloween mask. Each person must fish out an object from the pumpkin. As you create a friendly ghost story, you must include your object in the storyline, before passing it on to the next person. Make sure everyone includes their object as part of the story.

Invent Your Own Ending. If the ending of your story seems too frightening, ask your children to come up with their own. It's important to let your children feel in control of the story. Even if their own original ending is scary, it will be within the limits of what they can handle. It will also strengthen their imaginations and verbal skills. The most important rule? No violence, no matter how tempting.

Try finishing the following ghost stories with your kids.

Mark's Big Adventure

Mark always walked to school in the same direction. He skipped past the town post office, hopped over the stones alongside the river, then ran through an open field of corn before arriving at the small schoolhouse on the hill. But on this day, Mark was running late. He didn't want Mr. Medblocker, the principal, to yell at him, so he decided to take a short cut through the old abandoned churchyard at the end of Main Street. It was filled with old, crumbling tombstones and tall weeds. He walked across the front yard and over a patch of straggly daffodils when suddenly he heard, "Ouch! Stop stepping on me, will, you?" He looked down, and he couldn't believe what he saw.

My Friend, the Ghost

On Halloween, Naomi loved to dress up like a ghost. This year she convinced her neighbor Sally, to be a ghost, too. That way they could spook the whole neighborhood together. While the two were out trick-or-treating, they ran into Sally's brother on the street. "Hey Joe," said Naomi. "Want to join me and your sister?" "What are you talking about?" said Joe. "My sister is at home tonight, sick with the flu." "No silly, she's right here." But when Naomi lifted up Sally's mask, she . . .

Claremont High

Kids at Claremont High thought their gym teacher was a bit strange. For starters, occasionally he walked in the air. Once, the janitor caught him flying about the auditorium. Nobody minded much because he was such a nice man. Or was he a ghost? One day, the gym teacher said to a class of third graders . . .

Has Anyone Seen My Nose?

One morning Professor Pretzelmeyer looked in the mirror and screamed. His nose had fallen off! "How did that happen?," he shouted. He called to his wife, who entered the room. Something was different about her. She didn't look like herself at all. And even stranger, when she saw his missing nose, she . . .

Guess Who?
Normally, the movie theater was packed on Saturday. But today, it was empty. Only Susie and her friend and a strange man were in the theater. As the movie began, Susie heard the man approaching from behind. She turned around and . . .

Sneaky Sneakers
Shoes don't normally talk, but on Halloween anything is possible. Susie should never have bought new sneakers on October 31st, because when she wore them outside that day, they . . .

What happens if the children come up with an ending that's even more gruesome than the ones in scary books?

If you let your children create their own ending, they will be in control of the and narrative can get the characters out of trouble whenever they choose. Although the content of your children's story may not be to your liking, they won't feel victimized or frightened by the characters since they are the masters of their own story. However, I do draw the line with violence. What I've discovered is that children often use violence in a story to avoid participating fully in the creative process.

If we are weaving a ghost story about a character named Joe, for example, and one of my students continues the story by saying, "And then Joe got hit on the head and died," she's actually excusing herself from the hard imaginative thinking a story requires by ending it. I'll stop her and say, "No violence, try again. " Without fail, that student will come up with the most beautiful alternative to violence you can imagine. Storytelling isn't a natural feature in our lives anymore. Therefore, kids need that creative push. Saying no to violence in stories not only creates better narratives, but also sends an important message to our kids: *There's always a better solution to your problems than violence. You have the power to change your plot line. It begins with your imagination.* You'll be amazed by how readily they can become creative storytellers once violence isn't an option.

Following is a "jump tale" to tell your kids. Jump tales always end with a boo or a yelp or something that causes a child to jump. I like the following story because, while it is suspenseful and even a little frightening, it resolves itself playfully at the end.

Long, Long Fingers and Ruby, Ruby Lips

Origin unknown, retold by MARK PIERCE and KAREN JENNINGS

❃ Every day Eddie and I walked by the old Perkins house on our way home from school. The old Perkins house had been abandoned for years. All the windows were boarded up and the shingles were peeling. Everybody said the Perkins house was haunted.

One day Eddie and I were walking by the house when Eddie said, "I dare you to go into that house." I said, "I dare you to go into that house." He said, "I dared you first," and I said, "Well I dared you second." Then he said, "We'll both go in together." I said, "Okay, we'll both go in together. Come on."

Slowly we pushed open the gate—*EEEEEKKKKK.* We walked down the path that led to the front porch. All around us were weeds that had grown as tall as we were. We climbed the steps to the front porch. Loose boards creaked beneath our feet—*erk erk erk.* We walked up to the front door and turned the knob—*click, click, eeeer-rrrkkkkk.* We stepped inside. As we got inside, the door slammed behind us—*Boom!* It was so dark we couldn't see our hands in front of our faces. We reached for the door but it was locked. We were trapped. We started feeling our way along the wall when we heard someone breathing behind us. *"Haahh . . . Haahh . . . Haahh . . . Huuhh."* Then a voice somewhere said, "Do you know what I am going to do with my long, long fingers and my ruby, ruby lips?"

"NO!!!!" Eddie and I screamed. We ran and tripped into the staircase. We ran up the stairs.

When we got to the second floor, we saw light pouring out from below the doors in the hall. We went to the first door and opened it. Most of the boards in the windows had broken off.

We pushed the rest of the boards out. We were looking down onto the roof of the porch. I climbed out and started to crawl across the porch when *BANG*, my foot went through the roof. Eddie reached out and pulled me back in.

We went out of the room and down the hall to the next room. Light was leaking through the window. Most of the boards had been knocked out and a branch stretched across the window. Eddie climbed out this time and grabbed the branch. *BANG!* The branch snapped. I pulled him back in through the window, and we ran out to the hall again. There in the darkness again when we heard somewhere in the distance *"Haahh . . . Haahh . . . Haahh . . . Huuhh!"* Someone said, "Do you know what I am going to do with my long, long fingers and my ruby, ruby lips?"

"NO!" Eddie and I screamed. We ran straight into a wall.

I fell and grabbed a light on the wall to pull myself up. The lamp twisted in my hand, and as it did the wall slid open to reveal a secret staircase landing down to the basement. "Maybe there's a way out through the basement," we thought. The floor of the basement was all mud. Our feet went *squee squee squee* as we groped along the wall searching for a way out. The walls were wet with moss. The door upstairs opened. Someone came down the stairs. *Erk erk erk.* Feet *squeed* across the muddy floor. *Squee squee squee.* We felt someone's breath on our faces—*AaahhhhhhuuuAaahhhhh-huuu.* Eddie and I said, "No, what are you going to do with your long, long fingers and your ruby, ruby lips?!!!" And he said, "This. *Blublublublublu.*" (For the final *Blublublublublu* run your fingers over your lips and make the sound.) ❋

6

Who Towed Noah's Ark?

Bringing Bible Stories to Life

Some tell stories to help people to sleep.
I tell stories to wake people up!
RABBI NACHMAN OF BRASLAV

"No, you have it all wrong," replied the ten-year-old professor. "The Red Sea didn't part. Actually, there were these giant turtles living underneath the water. The turtles lifted up their backs and Moses and all the Israelites ran across their shells to the other side. But when the Egyptians came after them, the turtles sunk down under water and they couldn't get across."

"Thank you, Professor Mayonnaise, " I said to him. " It's an excellent theory. But Professor Pretzel, a noted scholar from South-field, Michigan, disagrees with you entirely. Are you here today, professor?"

Dozens of hands flew into the air. Every one of my sixth-grade Hebrew school students wanted a crack at interpreting the story of Exodus. "Yes, Professor Pretzel," I said, motioning to a freckle-faced girl in the back of the sanctuary.

"Actually," she said, mimicking a snobby, high-brow academician, "my research has shown that the Israelites surfed across the sea on surfboards." "Well why didn't the Egyptians do the same?" I asked her. "Because, they didn't know how to surf!" she exclaimed.

Suddenly, to my surprise and delight, a teacher raised her hand. "Who are you?" I asked. "I'm Professor Fluffernutter," she answered, and the class roared with laughter. "I think all of you are wrong about this. You see, I know what really happened. Macy's was having a huge 50-percent-off sale at the bottom of the Red Sea. All the Israelites pushed their way into the store, and there were so many people trying to get a bargain that they displaced all the water and it flooded over the banks and stopped the Egyptians in their tracks."

There was another explosion of giggles, a sound I relish, because I know when kids are having fun with a lesson, they'll want to return to it again and again.

When I look back on my own religious education, it is not with much excitement. It was pedantic and methodical, offering us zero opportunity to tap into our wellsprings of imagination. In the end, I have only two memories of those early days in Hebrew school: (1) drawing a picture of Moses, which we copied out of a book, and (2) winning a Certificate of Merit (I didn't know what *merit* meant but my uncle told me it meant keeping your mouth shut). It wasn't until I became a professional storyteller that I began to delve into the rich treasure trove of material that had eluded me as a youngster.

I love to tell Bible stories to kids. Because no matter how many high-tech, fast-paced movies they have seen, no matter how many thrillers they have read, no storyline can capture their imaginations more vividly than the Bible. Where else can you find a stick that transforms into a snake, a river that turns into blood, a boy who gets thrown into a well by his own brothers, a guy who ends up inside the mouth of a whale, a donkey that talks, a snake that deceives, a king who dreams the future, a woman who turns into salt, a sea that parts, and a bush that smokes but doesn't burn?

If you believe in God, they're great stories. And if you don't believe in God, they're great stories. But they're more than just examples of good writing. They can be our finest teachers, conveying life lessons, revealing human weaknesses and foibles, inspiring compassion and growth. They're like giant mirrors, forcing us to look at ourselves through the lives of those who came before, those whose emotional lives were no less complicated than ours.

Adam Sandler or Michael Jordan may be today's role model for young boys, but it wasn't long ago that Moses or Abraham won that coveted spot. "Bible stories were ingrained in us from an early age, and the people were so real for us," my Uncle Joe once told me. "Sad King Saul, brave Moses, suffering Jonah. These characters became like heroes for us, and the way they dealt with life and composed themselves, they were the best teachers. They're still in my imagination today."

Although the Bible doesn't have the same relevance in many people's lives as it once did, its stories are still one of our most important legacies. They're fantastic teachers, filled with humor and suspense, villains and heroes, wisdom and guidance. Whether you're religious or not, whether you even believe in God or not, the stories from the Old and New Testaments are riveting pieces of literature that, if approached correctly, will dazzle your children while stimulating their imaginations.

When I roughhouse with my son, Benjamin, I do it within a biblical context. So for example, he'll play Judah Maccabee and I'll be a Greek soldier and he'll fight me to defend the Great Temple. Or I'll be Pharoah and he'll be Moses and he'll look behind him, as if he's being chased, and he'll scream, "The Egyptians are coming!" Then he'll hide under the covers of his bed because they represent "the cloud of glory," a shield in the Bible that protects the Jews from

Pharoah's armies. I try to tear away the covers and pretend to give him a struggle, but I never pull them off completely because I don't want Benjamin to go away feeling unprotected. So many stories in the Bible are about the Jews being persecuted and I don't want him to think that they're always victims, always captured. I want to make these Bible stories personal to my son, not something outside of him. So that when he studies the topic fifteen years later, he'll feel as if he's going home again. He's seven years old now, and when the rest of the kids his age talk about John Elway or Howard Stern as their heroes, Benjamin talks about Moses and Joshua. These are characters with real nobility that I want him to emulate. I want to use these great stories to inculcate in him a sense of value and importance in something that matters.

ARYEH SPERO, father of Benjamin, 7

BACKGROUND

The Bible is divided into two parts: The Old Testament comprises creation stories and the stories of the ancient Hebrews, and the New Testament consists of writings about Jesus and his first followers. The Christian Bible is made up of both the Old and the New Testament. Because of my background and experience in storytelling, the stories I've chosen to work with in this chapter are from the Old Testament. These are the stories I know best and with which I have developed a level of expertise. However, the activities can be readily applied to any story in the Bible, whether it's from the Old or the New Testament.

SELECTING YOUR STORY

Which Bible story should you tell? Whichever one resonates with you. There are lessons to learn from all of the stories in the Bible, but if you want to be effective, you have to have an emotional involvement with the material. Choosing a story because you like what it has to say intellectually is fine, but don't be surprised if your kids don't get turned on by it. What touches you will touch them. What excites you will excite them.

There is an ample amount of death and destruction, bloodshed and gore in the Bible. For some children, hearing that the Red Sea turned to blood and that all first-born children were killed in Egypt may be hard to digest. Only you know your children's limits, so use your discretion accordingly. But the discussions you have after your reading can do much to alleviate the more frightening moments.

> Growing up Catholic, I loved having female images to emulate. . . .
> In particular I was touched by the women in the Bible who would completely abandon themselves emotionally in order to care for someone else. I was deeply moved by the way Mary Magdalene loved Jesus selflessly and the way she was completely renewed by loving him; or Ruth's devotion to her mother-in-law, and how she just dropped everything to care for somebody else and turned her life around in the process. These women taught me that by caring for others, you care for yourself. You find humanity that way.
>
> MARY CLEARY

Unless you want to read directly from the Old or New Testament, you can find the most popular Bible stories adapted in children's editions. Nine times out of ten, they don't have enough zip for me. I'm often frustrated by their lack of rich details and descriptions. That's why I've learned never to take most children-oriented Bible stories at face value. Instead, I see them as mannequins that need to be dressed. Naturally, I want to stick to the basic story. But I also want to fill in the gaps, providing visual imagery where there isn't any, giving voice to characters who don't have one, and looking for places where I can utilize audience participation.

PREPARING YOUR STORY

When I start to prepare a story for a performance, the first thing I do is read through the story two or three times. Once I'm comfortable with it, I then go back and ask myself the following questions:

1. What information is missing from this passage?
2. What am I curious about that's not mentioned here?
3. What part of this story lends itself to audience participation, including sound effects, physical movements, and dialogue?

Let's look at an example of how I might approach a Bible story using an excerpt from "The Queen of Sheba" in the *Illustrated Jewish Bible for Children* by Selina Hastings:

The Queen of Sheba had heard about the wisdom of Solomon, and she wished to see for herself if all she had heard was true. So she traveled a long way from the distant land of Sheba with a great camel caravan, loaded with spices and gold and precious stones, until she came to Jerusalem. The king received her courteously, and she asked him many difficult questions. But none was too difficult for Solomon: he answered them all.

While this is fine as a printed text, we'll need to add a few more images to make it work as a spoken word text. Remember, listeners don't have the luxury of going back and rereading a page or pacing themselves, like the reader does. Therefore, we must look for any opportunity to make the word become more visual, audible, and participatory.

Let's answer some of my earlier questions.

1. What information is missing from this passage? For starters, I'd like to know what Sheba looks like. Was she dark-skinned or pale? Did her eyes sparkle like emeralds, or were they dull and lifeless? By adding details such as these, you're making it more visual and, therefore, more accessible, for the listeners. You might change the passage so that it sounds like this: *The Queen of Sheba was tall and strong, with olive skin and shiny, jet-black hair.* Or, *The Queen of Sheba was a woman of such power that when she stared at you, your knees began to wobble.* Whenever there's a queen or a king in a story, I always try to have fun with the crown; for example, *The Queen of Sheba's crown was filled with so many jewels that if she turned her head too far to the right, she would fall down.* Sometimes, instead of a bejeweled crown, I'll fill it with silly objects: *The queen's crown was filled with three thousand hot dogs, and the mustard ran onto her nose.* As long as I'm not taking away or altering a basic storyline, I feel free to take such liberties. The more you turn your story into a moving picture, the more fun and effective it will be for your kids.

2. What am I curious about that's not mentioned here?

> The king received her courteously, and she asked him many difficult questions. But none was too difficult for Solomon: he answered them all.

Sheba asked Solomon many difficult questions to test his wisdom. What were they? You can have some fun by asking your kids to make up questions. Or make up some questions yourself and insert them into the existing text as you read aloud, and then ask your kids to answer them. For example, you might add the following questions to the passage:

> "What shoes should I wear tomorrow? The brown pumps or the crocodiles?"

"Do you think (insert name of your child here) will do well at school this year?"

"Will the Red Sox win the World Series?"

"Why is the world round?"

"Will we ever have world peace?"

3. What part of this story lends itself to audience participation, including sound effects, physical movements, and dialogue?

So she traveled a long way from the distant land of Sheba with a great camel caravan, loaded with spices and gold and precious stones, until she came to Jerusalem.

This sentence is filled with opportunities for the storyteller to elicit participation. Generally, any sentences that mention journeys or traveling can be expanded to include participatory activities. Were I telling this story I might say, "She traveled a long way from the distant land of Sheba, past three lazy donkeys who snored (get kids to make sound of a donkey snoring), past a sandstorm that blew them all over the place (mime being blown and getting sand in your eyes), past an oasis and a Bedouin with his flock of talking sheep (make sound effects), she traveled for days and days and days, until her camels complained to her of their aching toes."

If you're too tired to think or have worn out your imagination that day, simply let the kids do all the work. One of the most successful participatory techniques I've developed is called "Fill in the Missing Word." Simply stop the story at a specific point in a sentence and ask the kids to supply a word. It works like a charm.

Were I using this technique I would say, "She traveled a long way from the distant land of Sheba with a camel caravan, past a_____ (ask kids to fill in the word), over a _____, under a _____, through a _____, on top of a _____, and into a _____, until she came to Jerusalem.

The key is to *accept* whatever word they choose, even if it doesn't make perfect sense within the context of the story. If their answers are silly or too contemporary, accept them anyway. You won't affect the basic storyline but you will give them a sense of empowerment and a belief in their imaginations.

If you're concerned about historical accuracy, you can use this same "Fill in the Missing Word" technique to teach them, say, about ancient Arabia. Ask your kids to think about the kinds of things they might have seen from atop a camel if they were part of Sheba's caravan. Then fill in the words accordingly.

You may not want to embellish your texts to the extent that I do, and you don't need to. By merely adding the simplest sound effect, one descriptive word, or a short bit of extra dialogue, your story and your child's pleasure will be immeasurably enhanced.

> Until the present day, I can feel the greatness of those stories working in me, giving color, giving itself into my own way of thinking. Sometimes I'm really astonished to which extent it reached out into me, and this was completely without any other studies. So I would have to say it was the simple beauty of the Bible itself that became part of my makeup. Going out from school we would look for the right place to play. . . . We would talk about Jacob, what went wrong with him? We would compare him to our own fathers. You see, children when you let them be like this, together, warm with those beautiful stories, the lessons of them ring out, very sturdy, very sweet. Those Bible stories taught us how to live.
>
> Interview with SHMUEL GOLDMAN,
> from *Number our Days* by Barbara Meyerhoff

MODERN MIDRASH

Another technique that I adore when working with Bible stories is almost as old as the Bible itself. It's the creation of a Midrash, a story about a Bible story. The word *Midrash* derives from the Hebrew root *drash,* which means to explore or examine. Since the first rabbis, over fifteen hundred years ago, began weaving their stories, people have been trying to understand the meaning of the text by imagining what was happening behind every verse. Where was Moses' wife during his conversation with the burning bush? How did Sarah feel when Abraham took her only son to be sacrificed? How did Lot feel when his wife was turned into a pillar of salt? But even if you aren't interested in discovering the deeper meaning in each Bible story, creating your own Midrash will still be loads of fun for you and your kids.

Here's a Midrash that I wrote about the Garden of Eden. Being a New Yorker, I've told the story from a city dweller's perspective. In many ways, it says more about my own hopes and fears than it does about Adam's and Eve's. But that's the beauty of these original interpretations. They help us use the Bible as a vehicle from which to view our own humanity.

I call this story, "A New Yorker's Guide to Eden," but being an impatient New Yorker, I'm not going to start with day one. I'm going to start with around day four. That's when all the juicy stuff happens.

A New Yorker's Guide to Eden

And the Lord commanded the man, saying, "Of every tree of the garden you are free to eat; but as for the tree of knowledge of good and bad, you must not eat of it; for as soon as you eat of it, you shall die.
Genesis 2:16–17

❋ And God, being a hopeless romantic, knew life wouldn't be any fun without a moon. So God made a moon, and it glowed in the sky. But God needed something to howl at it, so he made a coyote. He tried a variation on that animal and came up with a dog. But the dog needed something to chase, so God made a cat. It was naughty and delightful and God liked it so much he made a larger one, a tiger. And larger still, a lion . . . then an elephant . . . and a dinosaur. When God was done with the large animals he made the small ones: ants, grasshoppers, bees, mosquitoes. And because God knew that one day there would be a place called New York City—cockroaches. But the moon looked lonely in the sky, so God created stars to keep it company. And they twinkled and glistened next to the moon. They were so enchanting God wanted to create something that was special and could understand and appreciate their beauty. That's when he invented Man. A handsome fellow named Adam, whose big eyes took in every drop of life. But quite honestly, how long could Adam swing from the trees, or feed the monkeys, or walk the dogs? He was getting bored. And he was lonely. So one night, Adam made a wish upon those stars. He said, "I wish for a human companion. Someone with whom I can share this beautiful place, someone who I can tan with in Miami." That's when Eve popped into the picture.

She was lovely and the two belonged to each other and Adam wasn't lonely anymore. They played games like hide-and-seek, leap frog, and Scrabble. They ran through the high sensuous grasses, danced among hot pink roses and speckled pansies, and dug their toes into moist patches of emerald dew. And they reveled in each other's company and this glorious paradise called Eden. Until one day something terrible happened.

Adam was off gathering food for dinner and Eve was sitting on the edge of a rock, humming a joyful tune, when suddenly, she was interrupted by a seductive, silver snake with a Mae West vibrato, which slid out from behind a tree.

"Sssssay there, sweetheart. What are you sssssssinging?"

"Oh, just a simple tune." Eve's words had barely left her tongue when the snake slithered up to her and said, "Ssssssay there, Eve. . . . Why don't you come with me inssssstead?"

Like the Pied Piper, whose music lured unsuspecting lads to war, Eve felt herself seduced by its serpentine sounds. She followed the snake behind a long skinny tree and was shocked by what she saw. The snake was standing beside a brand-new, shiny, green Apple computer.

"Sssay there, sweetheart, why don't you try this Apple?" The snake pulled up a stump alongside the computer and motioned for Eve to sit. Eve had never seen a keypad before and didn't know what to do at first. She cautiously pressed one key, then another and then another and another and another. Faster and faster, the pace was accelerating! Within minutes she learned how to do WordPerfect 6.2, how to type a mailing list of a thousand, how to fax. In short, Eve was obsessed.

Back in the woods, Adam was worried about Eve. He couldn't imagine where she had gone. Suddenly, he too was lured by the serpent's call. It drew him to Eve, who was hovering over her software.

"Why, Eve, it's Adam, your man! I've been worried about you. Where have you been?" But Eve was in no mood to talk. "Quiet, Adam, I'm busy. I'm programming the computer to figure out the maximum amount of animals we can catch within the smallest given radius." And she kept typing away.

Adam didn't know what to do. But the snake did. "Sssssay there, Adam, you handsome thing, why don't you try this Macintosh?!" And it too was as alluring as a ripe piece of fruit. And Adam also became obsessed.

And so it went. From that time on all Adam and Eve wanted to do was work on their computers. In the morning they would throw on their three-piece fig leaves and run through the woods to their stations—the woods they no longer took joy in. They would spend all day on their computers. The hot sun would shine brightly upon them, but they didn't stop to feel its rays. The savory scent of pine needles and pungent lilacs would surround them. But they didn't take time to smell them. And at night, when the stars twinkled in the sky and the moon covered them in moon glow, they were too tired to notice. And in this way, they could never again return to the Garden into which they were born. ❁

In the Garden of Eden story, I see many parallels to my own life. The tree of knowledge represents the choices I'm constantly struggling with: whether to succumb to the trappings of a high-tech, impersonal world that lures us into a false sense of security, or to turn away from that and have faith in something larger than ourselves. By not choosing the latter, we banish ourselves from Eden, if not literally, then metaphorically.

Creating a Midrash not only is fun for kids, but is also a tremendously effective way for parents to gauge what's on their children's minds. Many years ago I ran a storytelling workshop in a high school in Pittsburgh. I asked a group of students to tell the story of Noah and the ark from the perspective of dermatologists. They said, "As the animals walked on to the ark, Noah made his selections. The cool animals with long blond manes and perfect skin got to go to the comfortable deck upstairs, and the nerds and geek animals with zits were sent down below into steerage." Clearly their story mirrored their observations of school life and the often cruel and unfair treatment doled out to those who don't look or act a certain way.

Children can't help weaving their current preoccupations into their stories. Several years ago, during the week of the World Series, a boy at a middle school in New Jersey presented his version of the Adam and Eve story in the following manner: "Well, there was this snake and he turned Adam into a baseball, and then hit him with a bat, and the ball flew across the sky and fell through the roof of the school, and as it landed in its pew, it unfolded back into Adam."

I've also been amazed by some of the clever responses I've gotten over the years. During a workshop in London, one young boy and his father dazzled me by their interpretation of the Adam and Eve story, told from the perspective of dentists, by saying, "The snake was punished by God by having his legs cut off. So he spent the rest of his life, crawling on the ground, making the sound of the dental drill." Or the boy who told the same story as an insurance salesman, saying, "And Adam only had partial coverage."

Now it's your turn to have fun with the Garden of Eden story.

Write Your Own Midrash. Tell the story of Adam and Eve from the outlook of a

Shoe salesman

Lawyer

Fireman

Rock 'n' roll star

Dermatologist

Dog walker

Now do the same activity with Noah and the ark, Jonah and the whale, or any other Bible story of your choosing.

If your family is large enough, divide up into groups and act out the story as a skit. Or tell it as a simple narrative by passing the story along from one family member to the next. You can take fifteen minutes to put a story together, or you can improvise on the spot. Don't worry about whether the story ends up in finished form. The important thing to remember here is the process of exploring the story creatively. This activity works especially well for older kids, ages 7–14.

Use Inanimate Objects. By now you know that I love to use inanimate objects in my activities. Ask your kids to tell the Adam and Eve story as

> The Tree of Knowledge
>
> A clump of poison ivy
>
> A sunflower
>
> Adam's rib
>
> A star, twinkling over the Garden of Eden
>
> The apple

You can do the same with other Bible stories. If you've just read the story of Noah and the ark, ask your kids to tell you what they witnessed as a splinter on the ark, as an elephant's trunk, or as a mop that was constantly wiping up water on the deck.

Guess Who's Coming to Dinner? Pretend you're a food that Adam and Eve prepare for dinner each night. Tell your complete story, from beginning to end. What food are you? Were you picked, hunted, dug up, or grown? How are you prepared? Are you roasted, steamed, or eaten raw? Do you enjoy being that food? Who are your friends? What's it like being in the Garden of Eden? Have each family member do the same, and ask questions. The more questions you ask of each other, the better your stories will be.

A Trunk of Magic. Place an invisible tree trunk from the Garden of Eden in front of your kids. Have them pull out one object they might have found in Eden. Pass around a made-up story about the snake. Each time it's somebody's turn, they must include that object in their portion of the story.

Talk-show Madness. Become a talk-show host and interview Eve's nose. What did the Garden of Eden smell like? How about the apple? Have one of your kids portray Adam's ears. What did the snake really sound like? Was the Garden of Eden really quiet or were there sounds we don't know about?

It's easy to apply this technique to other stories. Ask your son to become Moses' nose and then ask him what the burning bush smelled like. Did he get a whiff of Mount Sinai? Make two members of your family Moses' sandals (the right one and the left one, naturally). What was it like trudging through the desert for forty years? Which sandal was the more sluggish one? Invite the whale that swallowed Jonah onto your show too. Perhaps he can shed some light on what really happened all those years ago.

I recently chanced upon this intriguing and timely interpretation of the creation story. It's particularly effective with older kids (ages 7 and up) and can lead to a wonderful follow-up discussion.

The Parable of the Serpent

Anonymous, from *Reading Between the Lines*
by PETER LOVENHEIM AND DAVID A. KATZ

*Now the serpent was more subtle than any beast of the field
which the Lord God had made.*
Genesis 3:1

❋ In the beginning, God didn't make just one or two people. God made a bunch of us. Because God wanted us to have a lot of fun, God said, "You can't really have fun unless there is a whole gang of you." So God put us in this playground place called Eden and told us to "enjoy."

At first, we had fun just as God expected. We played all the time. We rolled down the hills and waded in the streams. We climbed in the trees and swung in the vines and ran in the meadows. We frolicked in the woods. We hid in the forest and just plain acted silly. We laughed a lot.

Then one day this serpent told us that we weren't really having fun because we weren't keeping score. We didn't even know what "score" was. When he explained it, we still didn't see the point. But he said he would give an apple to the one who was best at play. And we'd just never know who was the best if we didn't keep score. Well, we could all see the point of that. Each of us was sure of being the best at play.

Things were different from then on. We yelled a lot. We didn't laugh so much. We had to make up new scoring rules for the games we played, and games like frolicking we stopped playing all together. It was just too hard to keep score.

By the time God found out about our fun, we were spending forty-five minutes a day in actual playing and the rest of our time working out the score. God was very upset about that and said we couldn't use the garden anymore if we didn't stop keeping score. God shouldn't have gotten upset just because it wasn't the kind of fun God had in mind. But God just wouldn't listen and kicked us out and said we couldn't come back until we stopped keeping score.

To rub it in, or get our attention, God told us we were all going to die anyway, and our score wouldn't mean anything. But God was wrong. My cumulative all-game score is 16,548$^{1}/_{2}$. That means a lot to me. If I can raise my score to 120,000 before I die, I'll know I've accomplished something in my life. And even if I can't, my life has a lot of meaning now because I've taught my children to score high. And perhaps they will be able to reach 200,000, or even 300,000.

Really, it was life in Eden that didn't mean anything. Fun's great in its place, but without scoring there is no reason for it. God has a very superficial view of life, and I'm sure glad my children are out being reared away from God's influence. We were lucky to get out. We're all very grateful for what the serpent taught us. ✺

Professors' Interpretations. My uncle Danny, an eccentric but brilliant man with a doctorate in physics, spends his days patenting wacky inventions and disproving theories. He disagrees with Einstein's theory of relativity, and to this day his license plate reads $E \neq MC^2$. This activity was inspired by Danny and others like him, who enjoy formulating their own theories and interpretations.

After reading a passage in a Bible story, announce to everyone that there's a professor in the room who disagrees with this part of the story. Then ask a family member to become that professor and share his or her theory. For example, the Garden of Eden story in Genesis never mentions the word *apple*. Perhaps your professor has a theory about what kind of fruit Eve might have eaten. During the Exodus story, ten plagues, including boils and frogs, are thrust upon the Egyptians. Perhaps your professor has his or her own theory about what the ten plagues really were.

> A cow tried to jump over the moon. But it didn't jump far enough and landed on Moses, who was floating down the Nile in a basket. Luckily, Moses was protected by strong twigs and the cow didn't crush him. But the cow did lick the chocolate off of Moses' forehead, that was left on him by his mother.
>
> DAVID, 9

DISCOVERING GOD

A man dies and goes to heaven. Once there, he looks down at his entire life by following his footsteps on a beach. Throughout most of his journey he sees two sets of footprints, his and God's. But he notices that during the most difficult, painful times of his life, there is only one set of footprints in the sand. Enraged, he says to God, "How could you have abandoned me during the hardest times of my life?! Look! During my most trying times only *my* prints remain in the sand." And God says, "Ah, but you're wrong. Those aren't your footprints. They're mine. I was carrying you."

Chassidic tale

Parents in my workshops often ask me for suggestions on how to convey the concept of God to their children. It's a complicated question, mainly because God is deeply personal and defined differently by every individual. Bearing that in mind, the following storytelling activities and stories can serve as a great starting point, helping you to begin a dialogue about God with your children.

God's Creations. Everyone knows that when it rains, God's angels are sending down a message from above. The next time there's a thunderstorm, listen to the raindrops against the window with your eyes closed. Pretend that the drops are really a secret code, sent by an angel. Decipher the code and explain the story behind it.

Thanking God. Pick out a photograph or illustration of a beautiful nature scene. Ask your kids to climb right into the picture, close their eyes, and listen carefully, raising a finger each time they hear a new sound. Do the same with smell, touch, and sight. Then ask them to tell you, or God, what they are grateful for at that moment. Make sure they stay in that picture and thank God for something within that natural setting.

Now ask your kids to imagine themselves in one of their accustomed settings—perhaps at a soccer game, a barbecue, or school. Ask them to describe everything they smell, touch, and see, while closing their eyes. What are they grateful for in that setting?

Fly on the Wall. Describe the prayers you hear in private moments. Become a fly on the wall of

A synagogue, church, or mosque

The inside of a car

The dinner table

A memorial service

What did people say to God? What do they yearn for most of all? Were they frightened? Grateful? Elated? What did they offer God in return for his blessing? Were people emotional? Did they seem bored or were they very excited by their prayers?

Biography. Become a biographer and tell the life story of one or more of the objects listed here. Talk about where and when the object was born, and describe its life journey.

Rosary beads

A prayer book

A prayer shawl

A skull cap (yarmulke)

A prayer rug

The following story, written by a Christian minister and author, Calvin Miller, is one of my favorites on the subject of faith.

Leonardo Lobster

from *When the Aardvark Parked on the Ark*

❊ It was senseless, but Leonardo kept charging the cage.
He was caught in a trap and he swam in a rage.
He knew he was done for and soon would be dead
When he suddenly thought what his father once said.

"If ever you enter a trap, Leonardo, you don't have
To find yourself stewed, baked, and dead.
You can't fight the trap, my two-pincered son,
By charging the steel that lies out ahead."

Leonardo grew calm and quit charging ahead.
His BB-like eyes raised up from his head.
He looked at the floor of his trap for a door
And clearly could see there was none.
But as he swam up to the top of his cell
He found the small window through which he fell.
He swam swiftly up, and rid of his rage,
He soon found himself outside of his cage.

"The reason all lobsters wind up in pails, with
Elegant people eating their tails,
Is that they don't try enough different ways
To escape from the prisons of men.
It does little good when you know you are caught
To keep charging at walls, again and again."

/ / /

Leonardo became a great liberator.
He moved through the
Traps and swam without fear.
Whenever he saw a brother entrapped,
He was careful, but unafraid to swim near.
"Look up, look up!" He would cry through the
Gloom, "Or this trap where you struggle
Will soon be your tomb.
The reason all lobsters wind up in pails, with
Elegant people eating their tails,
Is that they don't try enough different ways
To escape from the prisons of men.
It does little good when you know you are caught
To keep charging at walls, again and again.
Look up! Look up! Look up!" ✳

7

When Life Makes Us Blue

Stories That Address Childhood Issues

The Great Wanito doesn't drop around much any more. When I was a little girl, he was around all the time, particularly at my Aunt Lucy's apartment. She was my favorite older relative, an eccentric poetess who wore feather boas and sparkling hats and who had a passion for Native American folklore. The Great Wanito, an Indian mythical carnivore with an ominous, hypnotic gaze, would somehow wind up in most of her conversations.

If you disobeyed her, for example, and then stubbed your toe on her sofa leg, she would say, "You see, that's the Great Wanito, warning you not to argue with me." Once, when I talked too much at the dinner table, she turned to me and said, "You know, the Great Wanito only gives us a certain amount of words. Once you've used them up, that's it!" I suddenly saw myself in ten years, at age twenty, trying desperately to speak, with no sound coming out. The prospect of a wordless life was enough to shut me up . . . at least for that night.

I didn't always believe her stories, but they did affect me emotionally. Stories have a way of doing that. They seem to reach beyond the intellect and straight to the heart. They have a way of knocking on a door that needs opening, of inviting your fears, hopes, or deepest concerns to come out from their hiding places.

All children instinctively know how to put their deepest thoughts and feelings into their made-up stories. If they're worried about being abandoned, they'll become a loving parent who nurtures a child. If they fear the dark, they'll transform themselves into the sun and shine a light across the road. But children also know how to listen to stories and take from them what they need most. Stories help children connect to their feelings, even when they can't put them into words. They're like a soothing embrace—the message is implicitly understood.

The stories in this chapter are designed to help your children address common childhood anxieties, like a fear of the dark, the birth of a younger sibling, or the death of a loved one. They'll also help you tackle issues like thumb-sucking and feeling left out. I've tried to include stories that not only address a variety of issues but also represent a variety of cultures, including those in Africa, Ireland, and the United States.

These stories can help your children learn how to speak about feelings, how to trust their instincts, and how to make sense of all the new challenges in the world that they are facing. The stories will also remind your children they are not alone: others share their experiences and emotions. By observing the way characters in these stories handle familiar dilemmas, your children not only are arming themselves with knowledge that will help them tackle life's challenges but also are learning how to approach life creatively.

Of course, you should change and adapt these stories to fit your children. You can make the settings more fantastic or have them take place in your town, whichever will be more appealing to your children.

FEELING LEFT OUT

The Growing Up of Littleberry Johnson

by CARL FOX

❋ "You're not big enough," said the children to Littleberry Johnson whenever he tried to play in games.

"I am," said Littleberry Johnson, standing on his toes and puffing out his chest.

"You're not!" replied the children.

And away they ran, leaving Littleberry Johnson to kick at stones and chase his shadow.

One day he looked into the mirror to see how much he had grown since breakfast. But he looked just the same as always—not a bit bigger.

He looked into the closet and studied the shoes, hats, and clothes of his three older and bigger brothers. Suddenly he had an idea.

"Not big enough?" he whispered. And for the first time that day he smiled.

"I must start from the very bottom," said Littleberry. "Just like men start when they are building a house."

Taking off his shoes, he put on a pair of woolen stockings that reached above his knees. Then a second pair over the first pair. And a third pair over the second pair!

Over the stockings he put on a pair of rabbit-lined slippers. Over the slippers went a pair of shoes, and over the shoes a pair of overshoes, and over all went rubber boots!

Next came the pants. First he put on a pair of cotton pants, next a pair of woolens, then a pair of fleece-lined pants, and last of all, a heavy pair of corduroys!

Next came the vests—one, two, three vests. Then—one, two, three woolen sweaters. A bathrobe. A woolen jacket. A leather jacket. A woolen coat and a sheep-lined coat that reached to his ankles.

Around his neck he wrapped a yellow scarf and a blue scarf and a brown scarf.

Over his head he pulled two knitted hats and a fur hat tied with a red scarf under his chin.

And when he had put on no less than three pairs of woolen gloves, Littleberry Johnson looked into the mirror.

What he saw there was enough to frighten the bravest boy—or else make him laugh.

"Not big enough?" smiled Littleberry.

He slowly and heavily walked downstairs and out of the door and into the fields.

"I'll show them who's big enough!"

"What's your name?" asked the children as they ran to meet the widest and biggest and strongest-looking boy they had ever seen.

"Grumph—umph—bumphson," Littleberry Johnson mumbled in his deepest voice.

"Oh," they replied. "Oh, what a name!"

Littleberry Johnson nodded his head.

"Grumph," he said. "Umph—bumph . . ."

"We're going to have a race to the old mill," said the children. "Come on!"

"Well . . ." mumbled Littleberry Johnson. "I don't know. And besides I'm too big to be playing with such small boys and girls."

"Please," they begged. "Please play with us." And they pulled him by the coat sleeve. "Well . . ." mumbled Littleberry Johnson. "Just this once!"

"All right!" shouted the children. "Ready—set—go!"

Down the hill ran the children and Littleberry Johnson. But Littleberry Johnson felt twice as heavy as an elephant and his legs refused to run.

First he kicked off his right boot, and ran a few steps. Then he kicked off his left boot and ran down the hill after the children.

Next he kicked off his overshoes, his regular shoes, and his rabbit-lined slippers. But still he seemed to grow heavier and heavier. So off went his sheep-lined coat, and down the hill ran Littleberry Johnson.

But as fast as he ran, the other children ran faster.

The woolen coat was thrown into the brambles. The leather jacket, the woolen jacket, and the bathrobe soon followed the others. And through the woods raced Littleberry Johnson just a little faster than before.

Through the woods, around trees and fallen branches. . . . One by one he tossed off the sweaters and the vests and the scarves and the three pairs of woolen gloves.

In the middle of the cornfield, Littleberry Johnson puffed and panted and stopped.

Off came the fur hat and both knitted hats, which he put on the scarecrow, who was badly in need of a hat or two.

On the wooden fence he left the corduroys and fleece-lined pants. Onto the horns of a cow he tossed the woolens. And the cotton pants dangled from the limb of an apple tree as Littleberry Johnson swiftly flew over the ground and after the racing children.

With three pairs of woolen stockings to protect him from the stones and thorns, Littleberry Johnson ran faster than he had ever run before.

Over the stepping stones of the stream, over the stone bridge of the river, and up the dirt road that led to the mill he raced.

And one by one he passed the children as they ran to be the first to reach the old mill.

Before the creaking mill, Littleberry Johnson stopped. He stood with his hands on his hips.

"Well?" he said as the children raced down the hill and stopped before him, their eyes wide and their mouths as round as ripe apples.

"I thought you would never get here. And I ran only half as fast as I could have run—"

"Littleberry Johnson!" cried the children.

"What are you doing here?"

"Where did you come from?"

But all that Littleberry would say was:

"Grumph—umph—bumphson!" in his deepest voice.

"Littleberry Johnson!" exclaimed the children, walking around him, and looking up and down at him while he laughed and nodded his head.

"But where is the rest of you? We mean, how did you grow so large and so small again?"

"Come with me," laughed Littleberry Johnson.

And back they ran to where the cotton pants hung in the apple tree. Then they took the woolens from the horns of the cow and the corduroys and the fleece-lined pants from the wooden fence.

And piece by piece Littleberry Johnson put on all the pants, vests, sweaters, bathrobe, jackets, coats, hats, scarves, gloves, and shoes.

Then, standing stiff and straight and wider than any of the other boys and girls, Littleberry Johnson smiled and crossed his arms.

"Big enough?" asked Littleberry Johnson.

"Oh, yes! Yes, indeed!" said the boys and girls as they joined hands and danced around the biggest boy of all.

And that is how Littleberry Johnson grew up.

And that is why Littleberry Johnson no longer looks at mirrors or wonders what to do. For Littleberry Johnson is much too busy playing with his friends to worry about growing up! ✺

SIBLING RIVALRY

Dumb Baby!

by JUDITH BLACK

❃ Hi. My name is Jamil, and I am one, two, three, four years old. I like sunny days, I like ice cream cones, and I like my stuffed pet mouse, Frederick. But I do not like when it rains too many days in a row. I do not like it when my ice cream plops off of the cone. *Plumpf!* And I'll tell you a secret. I do not like my dumb baby sister.

And here's why. This morning I am asleep in bed with my five blankets, four racing cars, three books, two twin dolls (Raggedy Ann and Raggedy Andy) and my stuffed pet mouse Frederick. We're all sleeping real sound when suddenly we hear . . . the alarm! Fire! And out of the bed we all go tumbling. I leap over the five blankets and the four racing cars. I slide through my three books. I push past my two twin dolls (Raggedy Ann and Raggedy Andy) and land on my poor stuffed pet mouse Frederick. Sorry, it's an emergency! I run to the bedpost and grab my fire hat. I take aim with my plastic hose. But where's the fire? Hmmm. It's not a fire at all. It's just my baby sister waking up! Dumb baby. I made up a song about her. Want to hear it?

Dumb little baby. Dumb, dumb, dumb!

Doesn't know her finger from her thumb.

I just sing it very softly because my mom doesn't like it. I can hear her in the nursery talking to the baby. She says, "Sweet little honey, sweet baby. Let's change your diaper and put on your little polka-dot sundress. There, baby, jubba jubba joo. . . ."

Myself, I'm a big kid. I can get dressed without any help, you know. And I do. First my socks. One red, one green. I like it that way. Feels like Christmas all year round. Then comes my special turtleneck shirt. Excellent for keeping your neck warm like a turtle, but hard sometimes to get your head through. So I gather up all of the shirt to the top of the neck, then stick my head in very hard, and pop it up and out. Ta-da! I'm good at that! My arms go down these long tunnels. And here are my favorite Omigosh overalls. They have eight trillion pockets so I could put eight trillion things into them. But for now I just put in my four race cars and my stuffed pet mouse Frederick. I always wear my Omigosh overalls before my mom can put them in the wash. That way they stay real soft.

Now here is the hard part. I have to lift up one leg and I . . . I have to balance the other leg in carefully. Then while I balance on the careful leg, I step in with the other one. That's good. Then I pull them way up, but I still have to get the straps over my shoulders. So watch. I rock back and forth until the straps start to swing. Back and forth, and forth and back, like a teenager doing rock 'n' roll! Don't do this with the baby around, though. You might clunk her in the head with a buckle by accident, and your mom would get mad. So back and forth, and forth and back, then I grab one strap. Got it! Back and a forth and a forth and a back, and I grab the other strap. Got both! Then I pull the straps up over my shoulders. Clip one. Clip the other. Now I'm all dressed. Ta-da!

Uh-oh. Forgot my underwear. But that's OK, because right now my tummy is calling, "Time to eat!" I hurry to the kitchen, but my mom is busy with the baby.

She says, "Sweet little honey, eat your mashed bananas. Pleeease?"

Hey, I'm hungry, too! I point to my empty mouth. See, Mom? Ahhhhh. I point to my empty tummy. I thumpthumpthump it like this. I even faint and fall on the floor . . . Gaaack! Nobody notices.

Dumb little baby. Dumb, dumb, dumb!

Doesn't know her finger from her thumb.

But I am one, two, three, four years old. I can get my own breakfast. I can reach up to the drainboard and get my Spiderman bowl and my Bozo spoon. They're excellent for cereal. The crunchy granola is way, way back on the counter. But that's OK. Because I just got an idea. I pull out the bottom drawer and stand on top of it. I lean way over to grab the granola. I pop off the lid, turn it upside down, and pat the back. Oh. I spilled. But that's OK. You know why? Floors get hungry. Yes, they do.

"Jamil!" she says, "Jamil, did you make that big mess over there? I want you to clean it up right this instant!" Then she turns to the baby. "Now honey, you've got to eat your bananas. Please take a little bite of your . . ."

Dumb baby. I can clean this up by myself, you know. I don't need any help at all. Not like some people who just sit in a high-chair and say "gaa."

Dumb little baby. Dumb, dumb, dumb!

Doesn't know her finger from her thumb.

And I pull my bottom lip up over the top one to keep it from shaking. Then I ask Frederick to come out of my front pocket because now it is just the two of us for breakfast. A spoonful for him, a spoonful for me . . . and my mom looks over.

"Jamil?"

"Yeah? What you want, Ma?"

"Jamil, I've just seen what a big boy you are, getting your own breakfast."

I'm wondering if maybe she's not mad at me anymore. She kept going.

"And I just thought . . . looking at you . . . maybe there's something you know about eating that I don't. Like how to get this baby to do it."

I think I get it. "You want *me* to feed the baby?"

She does. "Please, Jamil, it would be a big help to me."

So I try. I take the bowl from my mom.

"Yuck. What is this stuff?"

"Mashed bananas."

"Gross!"

My mom smiles. "You ate them when *you* were a baby."

"That was before I knew better!" We laugh.

"OK, open up kid. Like this, Blaaaah. Look Mama, she took it! OK, open up again, Blaaaah. She likes it!"

"Jamil, she's eating from you!"

"She was hungry, Mama. How come you weren't feeding her?"

"Why, she wouldn't take a bite from me."

"That's because you didn't show her how to do it. You've got to open your mouth like this, Blaaaaaah. Look at her! Could you wipe her chin, Mama? The yuck is dripping down."

My mom says, "Jamil, you are wonderful. Do you think you could get up every morning and help me with this baby? I need you."

I say I will have to think about it. But I'll tell you the truth. Every morning from now on, as soon as the alarm goes off (the one that's not a fire, but just my baby sister) I'm getting up to help my mom with the baby. There are lots of things big kids know that babies don't. So I have to start teaching my baby. And I made up a new song. Want to hear it?

Dumb little baby. Dumb, dumb, dumb!

Here's your eyes, ears, nose and mouth and tongue.

Yes, there are lots of things big brothers can teach. And you know what? Now that her big brother is helping her out, my little sister is going to grow up to be very, very smart! ❈

THUMB-SUCKING

Slurp! Slurp! Slurp!

by ARTHUR ROWSHAN, from *Telling Tales*

✸ In a very faraway land lived a family of pandas. They looked just like other pandas, with black and white fur, pointed ears and flat feet with woolly soles. Their home was in a thick forest full of bamboo. Pandas love to eat bamboo.

During a very cold winter one of the panda families in the forest had a new baby. Mummy panda and Daddy panda called the new baby Peter. Little Peter was very cute. He would cuddle up in his mummy's arms and suck her breast to drink milk. When his belly was full he would sit in a corner and suck his thumb—slurp, slurp, slurp.

Everyone smiled and liked to see the baby panda suck his thumb. It was a sweet sight—a little baby, so cute, round, and fluffy, sucking his thumb. . . . He got all the food he needed from his mummy's milk. And when he wanted to be quiet and sleepy he would slip his thumb in his mouth and SLURP, SLURP, SLURP.

Gradually little Peter grew up. Now he was a big boy. He was not very good at using his thumbs and fingers for climbing trees like other young pandas. They would jump up on to a tree and wrap their thumbs and fingers around a branch or a twig to keep their balance. Then they would jump again to another branch and then another branch. They had fun, and roared with laughter.

Peter just had to sit there and watch them. Deep inside he really wanted to jump into those trees and wrap his thumbs and fingers around the branches, but he did not know how to. The other little pandas thought that he was lazy or not very clever because he didn't climb trees and play with them. Peter would hear them say to him, "Why don't you stop doing that?" or "Don't suck your thumb like a baby." When Peter heard them say these things he would get upset and angry. Sometimes it made him want to suck his thumb even more. He would get upset, angry and sad, and he didn't know why.

One day an old owl with a long white beard saw that Peter was sitting in a corner and watching the other children play. The owl asked him why he was sad. Peter told him everything about his thumb. The owl hugged Peter and said, "Be patient. Soon you will discover how to use your thumbs and fingers to climb trees." Peter became happy because he liked the old owl. He knew how wise he was. He could do many things.

Another day, Peter was sitting under a tree and watching the other pandas playing on a tree that was quite far away. He was sitting there and sucking his thumb. Just above him a little owl was jumping from one branch to another, just like the pandas were doing. Suddenly the little owl slipped and fell. Peter looked up and saw him. As he was falling the little owl grabbed the edge of a branch with his claws. Now he was dangling in mid air.

"Help!" shouted the little owl.

Peter looked up and said, "Why don't you use your wings and fly?" Soon Peter saw that the little owl was too small and his wings were not fully grown yet. Peter looked around but the other owls and the pandas were far away. He didn't have much time. The little owl's claws were slipping.

Peter did not waste any more time. He jumped on a lower tree and wrapped his thumb and fingers around a branch higher up. He tried to lift himself up but slipped and fell on the lower branch. He tried again, but fell again. The little owl was still dangling there. This time Peter tried as hard as he could. He wrapped his thumb and fingers around the branch. It was a tight grasp. He pulled himself up and stood on the branch. He had two more branches to go. He pulled himself up on to each of them. Finally, he was on the same branch as the little owl. He wrapped his thumb and fingers around the owl's little leg and pulled him up. By now the other owls and pandas came closer and watched Peter rescuing the little owl. They all cheered Peter on. "Come on, Peter. Just a little further." Peter pulled the little owl up and sat him on the branch beside him. Now the little owl was safe.

Everyone clapped and cheered. The old owl with a long white beard came and said, "On behalf of all of us I present you with this medal for your courage and the good use of your hands." Everyone cheered. Peter felt very special. He knew from now on that there were many other important and exciting things to do with his thumbs and fingers. Soon he joined the other little pandas jumping from one branch to another and had a fun time playing with them. ✱

CONTROLLING YOUR ANGER

The Dragon

by LISA LIPKIN

✱ No dragon's a dragon
　Without a big nose.
　It's long and its narrow
　Not unlike a hose.

Whenever there's trouble
And danger is near,
He uses his nose
To extinguish his fear.

He doesn't sniff with it
Or make funny sounds,

Or rub it or scrub it
When trouble abounds.

He sends out a flame
Often twenty feet long.
It's usually enough
To right *any* wrong.

The flames are convincing
They fly out with speed.
They're bold and uncold
And quite scary indeed.

You don't want to tangle
With fire from a dragon.
It'll leave you quite helpless
With barely a rag on.

But a dragon is gentle
When he's not afraid.
If ever you're hurt
He will come to your aid.

He's great fun to play with
Because of his height.
He'll fetch balls from trees
And see things out of sight.

He'll welcome you into
His cave or his castle,
And he won't flare his nose
And won't give you a hassle

A dragon is not
To be feared or mistrusted

Because on occasion
His nose gets combusted.

You see, deep down within us
We all have a fire,
Which simmers and bubbles
And wants to go higher.

But just like the dragon
Use wisely your flame.
'Cause playing with fire
Is a serious game. ✻

FEAR OF THE DARK

The Boy and the Dark

Adapted by LISA LIPKIN from an American folktale

✻ There once was little boy who lived with his mother in a small village near the Tombigbee River. There was no running water in his village. Therefore, it was his job to fetch water from the stream each afternoon. One day, he left his house later than he should have, and he'd never been out after dark before. He grabbed his bucket and started walking down the grass path, carved by generations of footprints, towards the crisp, clear stream a mile in the distance. Suddenly, he heard a familiar sound. "Ribit. Ribit." It was a frog, leaping away from the path, into a dense patch of woods. The little boy dropped his empty pail and ran after the frog, hoping to catch it.

But after an hour, the nimble-footed frog escaped the boy's clutches, and the boy returned to his bucket empty-handed. By now, the sun had begun to set. The little boy flew down the grassy path, filled up the bucket with water from the stream, and began his journey back. But it was dark outside now, with only a sliver of moonlight to guide him home. And the little boy had never been out after dark before.

There were many stories told in his village, stories that warned of the Hairy Man who patrolled the village at night and did terrible things to ordinary folk. The boy was frightened, but he knew his mother was depending on him for water and he couldn't disappoint her.

So he gathered up his courage and he began to feel his way down the grassy path. All of a sudden, he felt a presence in front of him. It was shining two lights directly in his eyes and crying out in a ghost-like, eerie voice. "What do you want, Hairy Man?" said the little boy, his voice quivering violently. But the Hairy Man wouldn't answer. "What do you want?" the boy repeated, and again there was silence. The boy picked up his pail and slowly inched past the Hairy Man, feeling his way down the path until he sensed that he was out of danger. But no sooner did he begin to relax when out of nowhere, a knife reached out and slashed his leg. "Stop it!! Leave me alone!" the boy shouted and ran as fast as he could, stumbling down the dark, scary path, as water flew out of his bucket.

After a while, he could see the faint silhouette of his house in the distance. And he breathed a sigh of relief, knowing he was finally safe from the Hairy Man . . . or was he?

No sooner did he slow down his pace, when the Hairy Man grabbed his ankles, forcing the boy to stop dead in his tracks. "Let go of me, Hairy Man! Let go and leave me alone!" he screamed. And he pulled and he tugged and finally wrenched his legs free and ran, all the way home.

When he arrived, his mother saw that all the water had fallen out of the little boy's bucket. "What happened son? Where is all the water?" The little boy began to cry and explained to his mother about the Hairy Man. And his mother smiled and wiped the tears off her son's face.

You see, the little boy's mother was very wise. She said to her son, "I won't make you go back out to get us water. But I want you to remember something. Everything you are afraid of can be explained."

And there was something about her calm voice, and the way she held him and smiled, that made the boy unafraid. He knew that without water the animals wouldn't drink, and his mother couldn't cook or wash. So he decided to go back out into the night to fetch the water his family needed.

He slowly inched down the grassy path once again. And sure enough, the Hairy Man was waiting for him with two bright lights, which he shone in the little boy's eyes, and an eerie cry, which he directed at the boy's ears. But this time, instead of running, the boy stopped. He remembered what his mother said to him, that everything you're afraid of can be explained. And do you know what those two lights were? The eyes of night owls! And that eerie cry, merely their "hooing."

He continued on down the path and again, something stabbed his leg. But this time he stopped. And do you know what those knives were? The prickly thorns on a bush!

He continued towards the stream and again, something grabbed his feet and held him prisoner. But this time he stopped. And do you know who was grabbing his legs? The roots of a big old tree.

He filled his bucket up and returned home. After that night, he was sure to fetch his water before the sunset. But every once in a while, his mother gave him special permission, so that he could go out late at night and enjoy the dark evening he had come to love so much. ✿

DEATH OF A LOVED ONE

This is one of my favorite stories dealing with the subject of death of a loved one, as it suggests that remembrance is a way of keeping those who were dear to us alive. In the story, a dead father is brought back to life by his sons. Although beautifully metaphoric, younger children may take this story literally. Therefore, you may want to reserve this tale for older children or have a discussion following the reading of it.

The Cow-tail Switch

HAROLD COURLANDER AND GEORGE HERZOG,
from *The Cow-tail Switch and Other West African Stories*

❋ Near the edge of the Liberian rain forest, on a hill overlooking the Cavally River, was the village of Kundi. Its rice and cassava fields spread in all directions. Cattle grazed in the grassland near the river. Smoke from the fires in the round clay houses seeped through the palmleaf roofs, and from a distance these faint columns of smoke seemed to hover over the village. Men and boys fished in the river with nets, and women pounded grain in wooden mortars before the houses.

In this village, with his wife and many children, lived a hunter by the name of Ogaloussa. One morning Ogaloussa took his weapon down from the wall of his house and went into the forest to hunt. His wife and his children went to tend their fields, and drove their cattle out to graze. The day passed, and they ate their evening meal of manioc and fish. Darkness came, but Ogaloussa didn't return.

Another day went by, and still Ogaloussa didn't come back.

They talked about it and wondered what could have detained him. A week passed, then a month. Sometimes Ogaloussa's sons mentioned that he hadn't come home. The family cared for the crops, and the sons hunted for game, but after a while they no longer talked about Ogaloussa's disappearance.

Then, one day, another son was born to Ogaloussa's wife. His name was Puli. Puli grew older. He began to sit up and crawl. The time came when Puli began to talk, and the first thing he said was, "Where is my father?"

The other sons looked across the ricefields.

"Yes, one of them said. "Where is Father?"

"He should have returned long ago," another one said.

"Something must have happened. We ought to look for him," a third son said.

"He went into the forest, but where will we find him?" another one asked.

"I saw him go," one of them said. "He went that way, across the river. Let us follow the trail and search for him."

So the sons took their weapons and started out to look for Ogaloussa. When they were deep among the great trees and vines of the forest they lost the trail. They searched in the forest until one of them found the trail again. They followed it until they lost the way once more, and then another son found the trail. It was dark in the forest, and many times they became lost. Each time another son found the way. At last they came to a clearing among the trees, and there on the ground scattered about lay Ogaloussa's bones and rusted weapons. They knew then that Ogaloussa had been killed in the hunt.

One of the sons stepped forward and said, "I know how to put a dead person's bones together." He gathered all of Ogaloussa's bones and put them together, each in its right place.

Another son said, "I have knowledge too. I know how to cover the skeleton with sinews and flesh." He went to work, and covered Ogaloussa's bones with sinews and flesh.

A third son said, "I have the power to put blood into a body." He went forward and put blood into Ogaloussa's veins, and then he stepped aside.

Another of the sons said, "I can put breath into a body." He did his work, and when he was through they saw Ogaloussa's chest rise and fall.

"I can give power to the movement of the body," another of them said. He put the power of movement into his father's body, and Ogaloussa sat up and opened his eyes.

"I can give him the power of speech," another son said. He gave the body the power of speech, and then he stepped back.

Ogaloussa looked around him. He stood up.

"Where are my weapons?" he asked.

They picked up his rusted weapons from the grass where they lay and gave them to him. Then they returned the way they had come, through the forest and the ricefields, until they had arrived once more in the village.

Ogaloussa went into his house. His wife prepared a bath for him and he bathed. She prepared food for him and he ate. Four days he remained in the house, and on the fifth day he came out and shaved his head, because this was what people did when they came back from the land of the dead.

Afterwards, he killed a cow for a great feast. He took the cow's tail and braided it. He decorated it with beads and cowry shells and bits of shiny metal. It was a beautiful thing. Ogaloussa carried it with him to important affairs. When there was a dance or an important ceremony he always had it with him. The people of the village thought it was the most beautiful cow-tail switch they had ever seen.

Soon there was a celebration in the village because Ogaloussa had returned from the dead. The people dressed in their best clothes, the musicians brought out their instruments, and a big dance began. The drummers beat their drums and the women sang. The people drank much palm wine. Everyone was happy.

Ogaloussa carried his cow-tail switch, and everyone admired it. Some of the men grew bold and came forward to Ogaloussa and asked for the cow-tail switch, but Ogaloussa kept it in his hand. Now and then, there was a clamor and much confusion as many people asked for it at once. The women and children begged for it too, but Ogaloussa refused them all.

Finally, he stood up to talk. The dancing stopped and people came close to hear what Ogaloussa had to say.

"A long time ago I went into the forest," Ogaloussa said. "While I was hunting I was killed by a leopard. Then my sons came for me. They brought me back from the land of the dead to my village. I will give this cow-tail switch to one of my sons. All of them have done something to bring me back from the dead, but I only have one cow-tail to give. I shall give it to the one who did the most to bring me home."

So an argument started.

"He will give it to me!" one of the sons said. "It was I who did the most, for I found the trail in the forest when it was lost!"

"No, he will give it to me!" another son said. "It was I who put his bones together!"

"It was I who covered his bones with sinews and flesh!" another said. "He will give it to me!"

"It was I who gave him the power of movement!" another son said. "I deserve it most!"

Another son said it was he who should have the switch, because he had put blood in Ogaloussa's veins. Another claimed it because he had put breath in the body. Each of the sons argued his right to possess the wonderful cow-tail switch.

Before long not only the sons but the other people of the village were talking. Some of them argued that the son who had put blood in Ogaloussa's veins should get the switch, others that the one who had given Ogaloussa's breath should get it. Some of them believed that all of the sons had done equal things, and that they should share it. They argued back and forth this way until Ogaloussa asked them to be quiet.

"To this son I will give the cow-tail switch, for I owe most to him," Ogaloussa said. He came forward and bent low and handed it to Puli, the little boy who had been born while Ogaloussa was in the forest.

The people of the village remembered that the child's first words had been, "Where is my father?" They knew that Ogaloussa was right.

For it was a saying among them that a man is not really dead until he is forgotten. ❀

8

Proud as a Peacock

Stories That Reinforce Positive Behavior

My best friend in college was wise beyond her years. One night, after I attended a small recital in which she had sung, she thanked me profusely and said, "You're a real friend." "Hey, it was my pleasure," I said, not understanding what the big deal was. "A true friend, " she continued, "isn't someone who's there for you when you're down. That's easy to do. No, I believe a true friend is someone who is there for your successes. It's much harder to do that for someone."

It's been two decades since she uttered those words, and yet they still have relevance in my life. Supporting someone during their successful moments is a hard task. It requires a generosity of spirit and an ability to remove yourself from your own ego for the moment. It also requires vision. It's often easier to recognize negative behaviors than to applaud positive ones.

The stories in this chapter will help you reinforce your child's positive behaviors. They encourage generosity and sharing. They teach us how to ask for help and accept people who are different from us. They show us how to trust ourselves.

The philosopher James Stephens said in *The Crock of Gold*, "I have learned . . . that the head does not hear anything until the heart has listened, and what the heart knows today the head will understand tomorrow." Stories move us emotionally, and therefore have tremendous power to affect our reasoning, helping us to change or reinforce our way of being in the world.

This chapter includes stories from around the world, from Jordan to China, from Egypt to the United States. Use them with your child as you would a goodnight kiss—its message needs little explanation, but its effect is everlasting.

HELPING ONE ANOTHER

Heaven and Hell

A Chinese tale retold by LISA LIPKIN

❋ Many years ago, a man decided to visit heaven and hell. When he arrived in hell, he was surprised by what he saw: Hundreds of people were sitting at an elegantly set dinner table. The most delectable gourmet foods—caviar, meat and fresh fish, cheeses and breads and desserts—were piled high atop the table. "This is incredible," the man thought. "Maybe hell isn't so bad after all."

But when the man looked closely at the diners he saw that they were all starving even though there were ample amounts of food in front of them. You see, each person had been given chopsticks that were five feet long! There was no way they could put the food in their mouths with these long chopsticks. To sit so close to a banquet and yet be unable to taste a morsel was hell, indeed.

Then the man visited heaven. On first glance, it looked exactly like hell. Hundreds of people sat around a beautiful banquet table, covered with the finest gourmet food. Here too, each person had been given five-foot-long chopsticks. But in heaven, everyone was happily eating the delicious food. You see, the people in heaven were using their extra-long chopsticks to feed each other. ✱

SHARING

The Two Friends: A Folktale

Retold by VERED HANKIN

✱ Once, a long time ago, there were two friends, Hassan and Michael, who lived near Mount Moriah, a mountain in today's city of Jerusalem. Hassan lived in an Arab village on the eastern side of the mountain, while Michael lived in a Jewish village on the mountain's western side. Hassan lived in a small hut with his mother, father, grandmother, grandfather, four siblings, uncle, aunt, and cousins. Michael lived in a similar-sized cottage with his mother. Every day the two friends would work from the crack of dawn until dusk, farming the land in between them. Together, they would pull out the potatoes, carrots, and corn from the ground. Then, each would take turns climbing on the other's back to pick apples and oranges from the trees. By the end of the day, they would round up baskets full of fruits and vegetables. These they would then divide into two equal shares, each boy taking home his share to his family.

Michael and Hassan worked hard. As soon as their heads touched their pillows, they would fall asleep exhausted. But one particular night, Michael could not sleep. He began to toss and turn, toss and turn. "Oh," thought Michael. "I keep thinking about my good friend Hassan. Every day Hassan and I work and laugh together. I can't think of a better friend than he. But poor Hassan lives with so many people. It just doesn't seem fair that we divide our crops into two equal parts. He should get more, because he has to share it with more people. I feel like a bad friend."

Michael continued to toss and turn, until suddenly he sat up with a smile. "I know! I'll take one-half of my fruits and vegetables and sneak them over to his barn. Everyone is asleep right now and no one will ever know the difference!" Michael leapt out of his bed, ran to the barn, and counted out half of his batch of crops for the day. Then, he tiptoed across the mountain to Hassan's village, sneaked the extra food into Hassan's barn, and ran back home to his bed, where he fell asleep, exhausted.

Meanwhile, back in Hassan's hut, Hassan was also having a difficult night. He too, began tossing and turning, tossing and turning. Hassan tossed and turned so forcefully that he woke up everyone in his family.

"What's going on?" squawked his mother.

"Why are you tossing and turning?" squeaked his grandmother.

"Go to sleep," muttered his grandfather.

"I wish I could," Hassan sighed. "But I can't. I can't sleep. I just keep thinking to myself."

"Well, quit thinking!" commanded his older brother.

"I can't," Hassan sighed again. He turned his head to the wall, but his mind raced with thoughts. "Poor Michael," he thought to himself. "He doesn't have a huge family like I do, one that looks out for me. When I grow up, and it is time for me to marry, everyone in my family will make sure that I find a bride and that I have enough money for a dowry. But who will look out for Michael? Except for his mother, he is alone. It is not fair that he and I take the same amount of fruit home after working together all day. He should get more. He really should get more."

Just then, Hassan sat up and ran for the door. "Where are you going?' his mother, father, and grandparents called behind him.

"I'll be back soon!" he called back. Hassan ran to his barn, sorted one half of his vegetables and fruits, and tiptoed to Michael's village.

He put the crops into Michael's barn, ran back home, and fell asleep, exhausted. In the morning, Michael rolled out of bed and peeked into his barn. He emerged, scratching his head in confusion. How could it be that he had given away one half of his crops, yet the amount seemed the same as before?

On his way to the field, Hassan also stepped into his barn and he, too, emerged confused, not understanding how he could have the same amount of crops as he had had the evening before. Both friends met on the mountain just as they always did, but on this morning each proceeded with great bewilderment. Neither friend dared speak a word, and the two worked all day long, silently. At the end of the day they divided the fruits and vegetables into two equal parts and each friend went his way, eager to give back to his friend.

That night, the two friends again secretly left their huts to deliver one half of their crops to the other's village. But in the morning, the two boys were astonished to find that their piles of food appeared not to have been diminished.

Hassan and Michael continued this way for weeks. But one particularly dark night, when the moon was only a sliver in the sky, each friend began to tiptoe to the other's village with one half of the day's earnings. Just as the boys reached the top of the mountain, they felt a giant *THUMP!* They had bumped right into each other! A cucumber went one way (*thud!*) and a tomato another (*splat!*) but the two friends were confused. Squinting to try to see amidst the blackness of the night, Michael squirmed, "Huh?" Hassan replied, "Eh?" Michael retorted "Hmmmm," and Hassan, "Ohhh." The two friends then raised their arms with a definitive "Aha!" and fell into a warm hug.

Many years passed. The great city of Jerusalem emerged on that hill, in place of the farm. When it came time for King Solomon, king of Jerusalem, to build the Holy Temple, he had to find a place worthy of the House of God. It was then that King Solomon remembered the story of the great friendship between Michael and

Hassan. He remembered, too, the spot where the two friends met and hugged, and that is the spot he chose for the Holy Temple.

The Holy Temple was torn down generations later. But the Western Wall of the temple still stands in Jerusalem in the Old City, right next to the beautiful, gold-capped Mosque of Omar. A holy site for both Jews and Muslims, the spot remains a sign of hope and of the interlacing boughs of peace and friendship. ❧

TRUSTING YOUR OWN JUDGMENT

A Bedouin Tale

Retold by LISA LIPKIN, based on one of Aesop's fables

❧ Long ago, in a small Arab village in the Negev desert, a Bedouin man rode his camel from his home atop a mountainous desert dune to the center of town, two miles away. His son accompanied him by foot. Some male cousins saw them pass by and mumbled to one another loudly, "How can our cousin be so cruel as to let his son walk the whole way to town in this heat? It's such a shame, isn't it?" The man felt terribly guilty after having heard their remarks and insisted that his son ride on the camel for the remaining length of the journey.

As they approached the *shuk* (marketplace) on the outskirts of town, they spotted a woman selling hand-woven carpets on the ground. As they passed by, she called out to them, "Some father you are. You let your child show such disrespect by letting you walk while he rides? What a disgrace!"

The boy felt so ashamed and embarrassed that he begged his father to join him atop the camel and ride together with him. "I don't believe it!" said the village shaman, when he spotted the father and son outside his tent. "You both should be awarded a prize for the cruelest men in our village! Don't you know that a camel that size can't support the weight of two of you? How unfeeling you are!"

The father and the son promptly slid off the camel's back. They purchased the items they had come to town for and began their journey home, each walking alongside the camel. As they passed the shuk again, a man selling colorful spices called out, "I've seen dumb people in my day, but the two of you win first prize! Both of you walk alongside your camel when one of you could be riding. What a joke!"

At that point, the man said to his son, "We've both learned a lesson today. You can't be swayed by everyone else's opinion. Hold fast to your own beliefs. In the end, it's your own judgment that counts." ❅

ASKING FOR HELP

The Mountain and the Cliff

by DAVID HOLTZ

❅ Once upon a time, in the Old Country (where all the best stories took place), there lived a man and his young son. The man was a merchant, someone who sold a little of this and a little of that just to keep food on his family's table. Usually he sold his merchandise to his neighbors in the town in which he lived. But once each month he would bring out his sturdy wagon, load it up with a little of this and a little of that, hitch his horse to the traces, and head off on a trip to sell his goods to the people living in other towns. And when he went on these trips, his son always went along.

Now generally nothing very exciting happened on these trips, but to the boy they were always great adventure. That was because the town in which he and his family lived was nestled in a beautiful valley, surrounded by tall mountains. And to get to any other town, you had to cross the mountains. And that was the adventure! For the only road out of the valley wound up and around the tallest of the mountains, and it was just barely wide enough for the horse and the sturdy wagon. And as the man and his young son rode up and around, they always had the mountain on one side of the road and a steep cliff on the other.

On this particular day, their trip started out like any other. Early in the morning, the father loaded his wagon with a little of this and a little of that. Then he hitched up the horse, he and his son climbed onto the wagon, and with a soft cluck of his tongue and a gentle shake of the reins, they were on their way.

All morning long they followed the only road out of the valley, as it wound up and around, and always they had the mountain on one side of the wagon and the cliff on the other.

It was almost noon when they came to the top of the mountain, where the road turned to begin winding back down the other side. The sun stood high overhead as they came around the last bend. And there, at the very highest point, the horse suddenly stopped! The father and son looked ahead, and saw in front of them a tremendous pile of rocks, which had rolled off the top of the mountain, right into the middle of the road. Rocks of all sizes! The horse had stopped because it didn't know what to do. If they had been on a road in the valley, it would have been a simple matter to pull off into a field and go around the pile of rocks. But here, on this road, they couldn't go around, because they had the mountain on one side and the cliff on the other! It seemed as though they would have to go back.

But the boy turned and said quickly, "Don't worry father, I'll get rid of all those rocks, and then we'll be on our way." And with that he jumped down from the wagon and began to work. He pushed rocks, he pulled rocks, he rolled rocks over the cliff. He worked for

two hours, and when he was done all of the rocks were gone—
except one. After all the boy's hard work, the biggest rock, the one
that had been at the bottom of the pile, was still sitting in the middle of the road. No matter how much he tried, he could not move
it. And even though he had been at it for two hours, and even
though he had removed every other rock, they were still stuck. For
with the large rock in the center of the road, and the mountain on
one side and the cliff on the other, the horse and wagon still
couldn't get past.

The boy walked wearily back to the wagon, wiping his arm
across his forehead. He looked up and said, "I'm sorry father, but I
can't move that last rock, and we can't get around it. I'm afraid we'll
have to go back."

His father looked down and asked, "Have you really done everything you could?"

Surprised by the question, the boy thought for a moment. Then
his face lit up with inspiration, and he ran to the back of the wagon
and got out a long piece of cloth, for they sold fabric. He went to
the rock, wrapped the cloth around it, took a deep breath, and
began to pull. He pulled until his muscles bulged, but the rock
didn't budge.

Disappointed, he walked back, slumped against the wagon, and
said, "I'm sorry father, it's no use. We'll have to go back."

His father tilted his head to one side as he looked at his son and
asked again, "Have you really done everything you could?"

Though he was very tired, the boy thought for a moment. Suddenly, his shoulders straightened as an idea came to him. He ran to
the back of the wagon and took out a long piece of wood, for they
sold lumber. He went to the rock, placed one end of the board
underneath it, and began to lean on the other end. He pushed
down with all his weight, he pushed until his eyes bulged, but the
rock didn't budge.

He stared at the rock for a moment more, then turned slowly

and trudged back to the wagon. Once more he said: "I'm sorry father, I just can't move that rock. We'll have to go back."

And once again his father looked at him and asked, "Have you really done everything you could?"

This time the boy got angry. "Yes! Yes I have! I have been pushing and pulling and rolling and throwing rocks for two hours. I've used the cloth, I've used the lumber. I really have done everything I could!"

His father shook his head, and said quietly, "No, you haven't, because you haven't asked me to help you." With that he climbed down from the wagon, and then he and his son walked to the rock. Together, they rolled it off the road and over the cliff. Then they climbed onto the wagon, and with a soft cluck of the father's tongue and a gentle shake of the reins, they were on their way. ❋

ACCEPTANCE

The Rooster Who Would Be King

by PENINNAH SCHRAM

❋ A long time ago, there lived a King and Queen and their son, the Prince. They considered this prince to be their jewel, their greatest treasure—the apple of their eye. The King made certain that the Prince had the most learned teachers and the wisest soothsayers to instruct him in all that a prince would need to know in order to be a great king, when the time came for him to rule the kingdom.

One day, a strange illness overcame the Prince, and he began to act like a rooster. He took off his clothes and roamed all around the palace, flapping his arms like a rooster and crowing loud and long. He also stopped speaking the language of the King and Queen. He ate only corn from the floor, like a rooster, and refused to sit at the table with others, eating only *under* the table *alone*.

The King and Queen became very upset and called for the best doctors in the kingdom to treat the Prince, in hopes of curing him of his illness. But nothing that the doctors and the soothsayers and the other healers tried seemed to make any difference, and the Rooster Prince continued happily crowing and flapping his arms, and hopping around in the palace, wherever he wanted to go.

One day, a wise old man came to the palace. "Your majesty, I would like to try to cure the Prince," he said to the King.

"Where are your medicines?" asked the surprised King, because all the doctors carried at least one bag filled with bottles of potions and oils.

"I have my own ways, Your Majesty," answered the wise man. "Allow me seven days *alone* with the Prince."

The King reluctantly agreed, since there was no other hope.

The wise man was brought to the Prince. The first thing he did was to take off all *his* clothing, jump under the table, and sit opposite the Rooster Prince. The Prince stared at the stranger for a very long time.

"Who are you, and what are you doing here?" crowed the Rooster Prince curiously.

"I am a rooster. Can't you see that?" answered the wise man, matter-of-factly but patiently.

"Oh, I am a rooster, too. Welcome!" replied the Prince, happy to have found a friend.

Time passed with the two companions crowing and flapping their arms.

One day, the stranger got out from under the table and began to walk around—a little straighter each day. The Rooster Prince had grown so fond of his friend that he began to follow him wherever he went. And the two roosters hopped around the palace together.

On another day, the wise man put on a shirt and a pair of trousers. "What are you wearing, my friend?" asked the Rooster Prince. "Roosters don't wear clothes!"

"You're right, dear Prince, but I was a bit chilled. However, I assure you, you can still be a good rooster even with clothes on. Try it," challenged the wise man.

The Rooster Prince put some clothes on, too—and continued crowing and flapping his arms.

The next day, the wise man sat at the table and ate some corn from a golden platter. The Rooster Prince sat next to his friend. The wise man signaled to the servants and soon the table was set with silverware, goblets, and golden plates. Slowly, the wise man began to eat all the delicious foods—in a proper manner—and the Prince began to imitate him. Soon a whole meal was eaten, and the Rooster Prince crowed most happily.

The following night, the wise man began to sleep on a bed. He again assured the Prince. "Don't worry, my Prince, you can be a good rooster just the same, even sleeping on a bed." And so the Rooster Prince resumed sleeping on his royal bed and no longer slept under the table.

Soon after, the wise man began to discuss the philosophy of life with the Prince. "Wait a minute, roosters don't have to think, and they certainly don't debate the merits of a way of life," declared the Prince. "Roosters just exist, being fed and cared for without any worries."

"You may be right," answered his wise old friend, "but on the other hand, it doesn't mean you can't be a good rooster if you do engage in discussion. After all, *you* will know that you are a rooster, just the same."

The Prince thought this over, and began to discuss philosophical ideas with the wise man.

On the seventh day, the wise man bid farewell to the Prince. As he was about to leave, he said, "My friend, remember—roosters are fair game for the hunter. So always try to pretend you are a human prince. Act wisely and help others. Farewell!"

From that day on, the Prince walked, ate, and talked like the prince he was.

And when, in time, he became a great King ruling over that entire kingdom, no one besides himself knew that he was still a rooster. ❀

Additional Resources

Storytelling Magazine is a wonderful resource, published by the NAPPS, P.O. Box 309, Jonesborough, Tennessee 37659. In addition to engaging articles, they also publish a catalogue and books and sponsor a national storytelling festival each October.

Here are some of my favorite storytelling Web sites:

www.storyteller.net This site features an amphitheater where you can listen to interviews with and new stories from storytellers from around the world, buy tapes, and learn of upcoming performances.

www.the-office.com/bedtime-story/indexmain.htm Advertised as the resource for busy business parents, this wonderful site features a plethora of traditional and modern tales for children.

www.lis.uiuc.edu/puboff/bccb This Web site for the *Bulletin of the Center for Children's Books*, reviews the latest children's books.

www.storyarts.org Story/Arts online is an educational Web site for teachers, parents, and students. Run by the professional storyteller Heather Forest, the site encourages the use of storytelling in the classroom and at home to enhance speaking, listening, reading, and writing skills.

www.storiesalive.com This Web site of the Boston-based storyteller Judith Black is filled with innovative activities for classroom and home use.

www.familyplay.com/stories This site features online Golden Books bedtime stories updated daily so you can print them out and read them with your child.

Here are a few of my favorite books about storytelling:

Bruchac, Joseph, *Tell Me a Tale* (San Diego, Cal.: Harcourt Brace, 1997). Drawing on stories from his own life, Bruchac looks at story in its many forms—ritual, celebration, rite of passage, history—and shows readers how they can incorporate stories into their lives.

McGuire, Jack, *Creative Storytelling* (Cambridge, Mass.: Yellow Moon Press, 1985). This book shows parents, teachers, day-care workers, and librarians how to choose, invent, and share tales for children, with an emphasis on fictional and traditional tales.

Moore, Robin, *Awakening the Hidden Storyteller* (Boston, Mass.: Shambhala, 1991). This fantastic guide helps you to get started on telling personal and family stories. It is especially good for those seeking a self-help path toward family building through storytelling.

Paley, Vivian Gussin, *The Boy Who Would Be a Helicopter: The Uses of Storytelling in the Classroom* (Cambridge, Mass.: Harvard University Press, 1990). This is not a how-to book. The author's brilliant personal essay on the way she uses storytelling in her classroom is inspirational and provides an invaluable window on the highly effective ways storytelling can be used to address the emotional needs of children.

Pelowski, Anne, *The Family Storytelling Handbook* (New York: Macmillan, 1987). The author shows readers how to use stories, anecdotes, rhymes, paper, and handkerchiefs to enrich family traditions.

Sawyer, Ruth, *The Way of the Storyteller* (New York: Viking, 1942). If you cherish great writing, this book is a must. Although written in 1942, the author, who worked as a professional storyteller and folklorist, drops pearls of wisdom that transcend time, instructing readers in the art of storytelling and freeing the imagination. The book also includes eleven of the author's best-loved stories.

Taylor, Daniel, *The Healing Power of Stories* (New York: Doubleday, 1996). This is one of my all-time favorite spiritual books on the nature of storytelling and its relevance in our lives.

Here are some great collections of stories:

Abraham, Roger D., *Afro-American Folktales* (New York: Pantheon, 1985). Great stories for ages 8 and up.

Courlander, Harold, and George Herzog, *The Cow-tail Switch and Other West African Stories* (New York: Henry Holt, 1947). A wonderful collection of West African tales that can be used to address adoption, death, justice, and compassion.

Gellman, Mark, *Does God Have a Big Toe?* (New York: HarperCollins, 1989). This book is a delightfully original collection of stories about stories in the Bible.

Jaffee, Nina, and Steve Zeitlin, *The Cow of No Color: Riddle Stories and Justice Tales from World Traditions* (Henry Holt, 1998). Children get to guess the outcome of each of these fascinating stories relating to justice.

McDonald, Margaret Read, *Twenty Tellable Tales* (New York: H. W. Wilson, 1985). This great collection of stories is for either teachers or parents and is filled with the author's notes about the history of each story and her approach to telling them.

Schulman, Janet, *The 20th Century Children's Book Treasury* (New York: Knopf, 1998). This book contains forty-four of the most memorable and beloved children's books, including *Goodnight, Moon; Where the Wild Things Are;* and *Madeline.*

Schwartz, Howard, *Lilith's Cave* (New York: Oxford University Press, 1988). A fascinating exploration into the darker side of Jewish folklore, including Lilith and demon stories from sixteenth-century Germany.

Torrence, Jackie, *Jackie Tales* (New York: Avon, 1998). Brimming with her thoroughly unique renditions of traditional and original stories, the author, a professional storyteller, also provides wonderful tips for telling each of her stories.

Credits

Black, Judith, *Dumb Baby*. Reprinted by permission of the author.

Courlander, Harold, and George Herzog, "The Cow-tail Switch" from *The Cow-tail Switch and Other West African Stories*. Copyright 1947. Reprinted by permission of Herny Holt.

Fox, Carl, "The Growing Up of Littleberry Johnson" from the *Golden Story Treasury*. Copyright 1951. Reprinted by permission of Golden Books, Inc.

Gardner, Richard, "Cinderelma" from *Fairy Tales for Today's Children*. Reprinted by permission of the author.

Gorden, Lisa, *Cow Painting Alongside Saturn*. Reprinted by permission of the author.

Hankin, Vered, retelling of *The Two Friends: A Folktale*. Reprinted by permission of Vered Hankin.

Holtz, David, *The Mountain and the Cliff*. Reprinted by permission of the author.

Miller, Calvin A., "Leonardo Lobster" from *When the Aardvark Parked on the Ark*. Reprinted by permission of the author.

Pierce, Mark, and Karen Jennings, retelling of *Long, Long Fingers and Ruby, Ruby Lips*. Reprinted courtesy of Mark Pierce and Karen Jennings.

Piper, Watty, from *The Little Engine That Could*, illust. by Ruth Sanderson, copyright © 1960 by The Platt & Munk Co., Inc. Used by permission of Platt & Munk, Publishers, a division of Grossett & Dunlap, a division of Penguin Putnam Inc.

Rowshan, Arthur, "Slurp, Slurp, Slurp" from *Telling Tales*. Copyright © 1997. Reprinted by permission of Oneworld Publications.

Schimmel, Nancy, "A Story for Heather" from *Just Enough to Make a Story*. Copyright ©1992. Reprinted by permission of Sisters' Choice Recordings and Books.